# DARK MANIPULATION
# AND PERSUASION

# DARK MANIPULATION AND PERSUASION

To Get Better In Your Life: learn and improve the art of Dark Psychology, Emotional Influence, Hypnosis, Analyze People and Mind Control Techniques.

Donald Goleman - Jake Greene

# Dark Manipulation and Persuasion

**Copyright © 2020 by Donald Goleman - Jake Greene**



ISBN: 9798683111656

Cover design by TheSkyDesigner

First Edition: August 2020

*You are co-creator
of your life.
The real power lies in you,
loved and strengthen it
incessantly.*

# Contents

**PLEASE**

*If you will like this book and want more quality books, we will really appreciate your review on Amazon.*
*The number of reviews a book accumulates on a daily basis has a direct impact on how it sells, so leaving a review, no matter how long, helps us keep writing quality books.*

**Thank you so much and good reading.**

# Introduction

*"Knowing your own darkness is the best method for dealing with the darknesses of other people."*

| Carl Gustav Jung |

The Have you ever gone into a confrontation feeling so sure in yourself, then walk out feeling confused but with no good reason why the other person should persuade you? Have you ever come out of a discussion promising to do something for another, but couldn't find out why you first agreed? You've manipulated chances. If you were playing with your feelings or using convincing words, you were raised to believe in or act on something you originally were not completely comfortable with. Before you started the discussion, you should be completely persuaded and so sure of yourself, but halfway, you found yourself forgetting thoughts, frustrated, frazzled and disoriented.

Manipulation can feel manipulated and leave you in doubt about your own abilities. Being continually manipulated will leave you angry, demoralized and despondent and wonder how you have not seen this coming.

Nevertheless, might you have stopped it, if you knew how to identify the indications that mean that someone may not be good?

Psychology is defined as the study of science behind every human being's thought, emotions and actions based on their own personal history or inclination to learned or developed behavior. In other words, people studying psychology are driven by curiosity and searching for knowledge on why people are the way we are. Dark Psychology brings this research into the secret parts of the human mind, the places that people are seeking to avoid, hide or conceal (if they even know about them).

Others use their experience with dark psychological tactics to influence others' emotions, gain control over others, or persuade people to do as they are told, often without ever suspecting their own emotions or acts. Some of the most frequently read and discussed sub-sections of Dark Psychology include: cyberstalking and other virtual predatory behavior.

This category also includes personalities as mild as web trolls on social media sites to the most severe as virtual identity thief's Political psychology falls into the realm of Dark Psychology, depending on who is the subject of the study. Those who have made lasting marks of the entertainment industry and those who dominate many artistic careers have thanked persuasion and reading people's psychological tactics for furthering their success in chosen fields.

The experience of each person with Dark Psychology in their personal lives all depends on the personality of an individual and whether they are the type to try to keep themselves from being the victims of dark psychological techniques or whether they are the type to use them on others as a way to advance their own position, to benefit from a certain situation or to knowingly cause harm.

What does the man who kicks the dog possess when a culture that worries of his life frustrate him? What feelings does he release at that moment when the dog screeches and howls in pain and fright? Why does he smile and wish further harm to the dog and enjoy the sight of an animal in pain? On-lookers are appalled by his actions and compassion for the defenseless dog this guy has been attempting to handle cruelly and without empathy for. Who is that guy? Why every now and then he's us all.

We all lose our sense of psychological equilibrium and rational thinking as we discuss the injustice or lack of opportunity in life. In the other side-wait-for this man to be wealthy, to have satisfied all his needs, and he still takes great joy in kicking and watching the dog suffer at his hands.

A sense of superiority in his ability to cause misery and the satisfaction of feeling superior to other lower-minded people whom he sees as unable to do what they want and therefore end up with his workers and servants. This superior situational thought leads to a lack of sympathy or empathy for others as just fools embracing his kind of superiority as leaders and legislators.

Manipulators exercise their power to manipulate and reap benefits from you by manipulating your feelings and distorting your mental beliefs. They are preying on your vulnerabilities and taking advantage of you by communication tactics designed to confuse you so that before it's too late you don't see what they are. Identifying whether you are being manipulated to shield yourself from being abused is critical, and promoting a healthy balance of power in relationships. And it begins with learning how to  evaluate the men.

# CHAPTER 1

# Delving into Dark Psychology

WE DEFINE DARK PSYCHOLOGY AS THE ART and science focusing on mind control and manipulation. Psychology, as a general term, aims at studying and understanding human behavior. It is focused on our thoughts, actions, and the way we interact with each other.

Dark psychology, however, just focuses on the kinds of thoughts and actions that are predatory in nature. Dark psychology examines the tactics used by malicious people to motivate, persuade, manipulate, or coerce others into acting in ways that are beneficial to themselves, and potentially detrimental to the other person.

The best definition for dark psychology is that it is the study of a human status in its connection to the people's psychological nature to prey upon other people. The entire humanity possesses a certain potential to victimize not only their fellow human beings but also other living creatures. Whereas, other individuals who might want to sublimate or restrain this kind of tendency, there are also others who opt to act upon some of these impulses. What dark psychology seeks to achieve is to make one understand those perceptions, feelings, and thoughts that end up leading to the predatory behavior of human beings. Dark psychology assumes this type of production is done for a given purpose and contains certain goal-oriented and rational motivation nearly all the time. The remaining portion of this time is essentially the dangerous victimization of other people with no purposive intent. In other words, we can perceive and define it by both religious doctrine and evolutionary science.

The point of dark psychology, as a subject, is to try to understand those thoughts, feelings, and perceptions that cause people to behave in predatory ways towards each other. Experts in dark psychology work under the assumption that the vast majority of human predatory actions are purposeful. In other words, most individuals who prey on others (99.99%) do it for specific reasons, while the remaining people (0.01%) do it for no reason at all.

The assumption is that when people do evil things, they have specific motivations, some of which may even be completely rational from their point of view. People do bad things with specific goals in mind and specific rationales for their actions, and only a tiny fraction of the population brutally victimizes others without a purpose that can be reasonably explained by either evolutionary science or some form of religious dogma.

You have heard many times that everyone has a dark side. All cultures and belief systems acknowledge this dark side to some extent. Our society refers to it as "evil" while some cultures and religions have gone so far as to create mythical beings to whom they attribute that evil (the devil, Satan, demons, etc.). Experts in dark psychology posit that there as some among us who commit the worst kinds of evil, for purposes that are unknown. While most people may do evil things to gain power, money, retribution, or for sexual purposes, there are those who do evil things because that's just who they are. They commit acts of horror for absolutely no reason. In other words, their ends don't justify their means; they cause harm for its own sake.

Dark psychology is rooted in 4 dark personality traits. These traits are; narcissism, Machiavellianism, psychopathy, and sadism. People with such traits tend to act in ways that are pointlessly harmful to others.

The skills and methods of influencing others can be quite different. They can be used both for constructive purposes and for various frauds. The characteristics of those who manage to influence people, no matter what is the "dark" in the dark psychology name.

People who successfully use dark psychology have understood fully all aspects of normal psychology. Thus, they understand themselves as well as others around them. They easily analyze others with this skill. They perceive the views, opinions and other information from those whom they wish to influence. Such a skill can be developed independently.

Certain stories of deception of citizens with the help of dark psychology, like those that were told at the beginning, were perceived as exotic, and the victims of this deception were considered unlimited simpletons. The bulk of fraudulent "exploits" using dark psychology as a special state of the psyche was not associated at all: the victim of dark psychological influence simply could not find an explanation for what happened.

As has been noted more than once, the specifics of dark psychology make the active user "process" the client in a roundabout way. He does not give direct commands to do this or that but encourages a person to do it as if he is acting on his own initiative. The person comments, asks, consults and - gets his way.

Behind his behavior is a certain strategy. One of them is speculation. The phrase stands in such a way that some phenomenon, action or object is presented in it as if it was actually accepted. For example, they ask you: "Will you pay in dollars or bitcoins?" The question is innocent, but you have not yet said that you intend to purchase this thing at all. The question assumes that you have already made such a decision and it remains to solve the trifle - to pay in bitcoins or dollars, about which you begin to reflect.

I suppose that what was read caused the reader an ironic smile: a primitive ploy, visible, as they say, with the naked eye. Do not rush to conclusions. Let me remind you that the "seller" has already adjusted to you and leads you, your consciousness is no longer as critical as when reading these lines. This is the basis of analyzing people first, then thinking steps ahead of them, even about their own actions and reactions.

The essence of this technique is as follows: the dark psychologist makes up the text of the suggestion, and then "dissolves" it in a story of neutral content. During the conversation, the "user" in some way selects the words of suggestion and they turn out to be a brilliant trap for consciousness. He (or she) will change the volume of speech, pause in characteristic places, speed up or slow down the story.

There are other tools for highlighting words and phrases in order to consolidate them in the subconscious. The "user" can emphasize the right places in the story with gestures, facial expressions, touching your arm, shoulder, back. He can approach you sharply, turn around, turn away, etc. All these manipulations, if you follow them, are the basis of dark psychology. Now let's think about how often this is done to us against our will. And how this new knowledge is about to turn your life around. But first, it is worth considering the various personality types you should get ready to come across...

# Theoretical Overview

The human condition related to the psychodynamics of those who prey upon others in a way that is motivated by deviant methods is known as dark psychology. Throughout, you are going to be studying bits of dark psychology because it can help you further understand mind control and how it works.

Virtually every human has the ability to tap into dark psychology. This may sound somewhat terrifying, since dark psychology is often known to be the psychology fostered by psychopaths and sociopaths, and it can be the entire foundation for how many major crimes are committed. However, for the purpose of this topic, you are going to learn about dark psychology and how you can use it to your benefit without compromising your own wellbeing, as well as how you can use the understanding of dark psychology to prevent yourself from being brainwashed by others.

The majority of dark psychology is based in goal-oriented motivation that can be rationalized by the individual who is completing the activities. Dark psychology includes the thoughts, feelings, and perceptions fostered by those who are responsible for using dark psychology to complete certain actions.

A lot of the forms of mind control are considered to be rooted in dark psychology because many believe that mind control is an impure strategy used by those who cannot be bothered to do things themselves. They believe that it is a form of evil, hence why it is called "dark" psychology. While we certainly do not want to alleviate the blame from true criminals, you should understand that you are not a criminal for using mind control strategies.

Mind control in this day and age can be a powerful way to encourage people to do the things you need or want them to do. Obviously, this type of powerful strategy can be used to have people do bad things or to create criminal results, but it can also be used to encourage positive results. The way this method works for you is entirely up to you. If you choose to use these strategies to justify and execute criminal behaviors, then you are going to become a criminal and you will likely end up prosecuted as such.

However, if you use these strategies to benefit yourself and those around you without doing harm unto anyone, then there truly is nothing wrong with using mind control to get what you want. There are many people who use mind control for various purposes, such as selling, building businesses, encouraging employees to do what they should be doing in order to keep a business running well, encouraging people to see past their fears and limitations, and much more. Being able to control someone's mind leaves you with a lot of power to do many positive things. Just as much power as you have to do evil things, even. How you choose to use your skillset is entirely up to you.

# Practical and Historical Overview

Mind control has a massive history in society. There are many parts of human history where mind control was used to create desired outcomes. It has been used to assist in exorcisms, possession, and healing mental illnesses in the past.

One of the earliest known forms of mind control was a technique called trephining. This technique involves a tactic where a hole was cut into the skull of a person who was believed to be possessed by evil spirits. It was believed that by cutting the skull open, the hole would enable evil spirits to leave the body. In various parts of the world, an instrument was pushed into the hole to "scare" the spirit away. This technique is essentially the earliest form of a lobotomy. Trephining was believed to be done all around the world as there have been many skulls uncovered from various areas of ancient civilization that feature holes on the cranium.

However, back in those times it was believed to be possible and so individuals would be subjected to brainwashing techniques to attempt to redeem their spirit and return their purity to them. In modern ages, we can suspect that most of these individuals were actually those dealing with mental illness and this was the best way that the society knew how to handle the situation at the time.

As a result of these beliefs, there have been many mind control strategies enforced over the centuries. Straitjackets, shock treatment, seclusion and sensory deprivation, rush chairs, restraining chairs, rotating chairs, and tranquilizing chairs were all some of the more harmful strategies that were enforced as an attempt to brainwash these individuals and return them to normal standards of thinking and behaving. Of course, these days very few of these strategies are used any longer, and there are many statutes of limitations on how the ones that are still used can actually be used. Furthermore, you don't want to be using any of these in your own brainwashing strategies because they likely won't work.

# CHAPTER 2

# Understanding Dark Personalities

Dark psychology is not a single, universally applicable medical diagnosis that can be applied across all cases of deviant personalities. There are, in fact, a wide variety of ways that dark psychology may manifest itself in someone's psychological and behavioral makeup. There is no absolute division of one deviant personality type from another, and many deviant personalities with prominent features of dark psychology may display elements of more than one manifestation of dark psychology.

We will explore three types of dark psychology personalities. It is important to remember that although the internet has spawned a huge growth in problems resulting from dark psychology, these traits have been part of human culture since ancient times. In fact, one of the dark psychology profiles we will explore here, Machiavellianism, takes its name from a medieval politician. Another, narcissism, takes its name from an ancient mythological character. Together, the three dark psychology profiles talked about here—psychopathy, Machiavellianism, and narcissism—make up what is known as "the Dark Triad."

# The Dark Triad Personalities

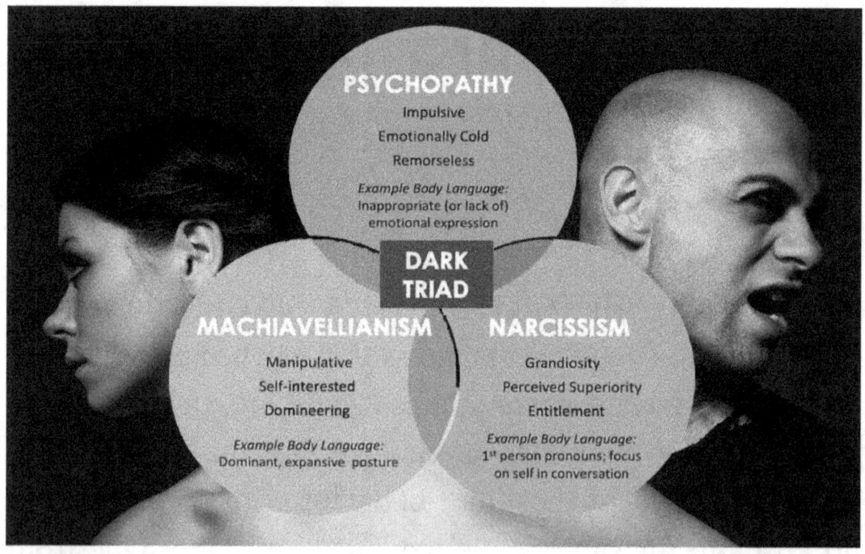


# 1. Narcissism

The term "narcissism" originates from an ancient Greek myth about Narcissus, a young man who saw his reflection in a pool of water and fell in love with the image of himself. In clinical psychology, narcissism as an illness was introduced by Sigmund Freud and has continually been included in official diagnostic manuals as a description of a specific type of psychiatric personality disorder.

In psychology, narcissism is defined as a condition characterized by an exaggerated sense of importance, an excessive need for attention, a lack of empathy, and, as a result, dysfunctional relationships. Commonly, narcissists may outwardly display an extremely high level of confidence, but this façade usually hides a very fragile ego and a high degree of sensitivity to criticism. There is often a large gulf between a narcissist's highly favorable view of himself or herself, the resulting expectation that others should extend to him or her favors and special treatment, and the disappointment when the results are quite negative or otherwise different. These problems can affect all areas of the narcissist's life, including personal relationships, professional relationships, and financial matters.

As part of the Dark Triad, those who exhibit traits resulting from Narcissistic Personality Disorder (NPD) may engage in relationships characterized by a lack of empathy. For example, a narcissist may demand constant comments, attention, and admiration from his or her partner, but will often appear unable or unwilling to reciprocate by displaying concern or responding to the concerns, thoughts, and feelings of his or her partner.

Narcissists also display a sense of entitlement and expect excessive reward and recognition, but usually without ever having accomplished or achieved anything that would justify such feelings. There is also a tendency toward excessive criticism of those around him or her, combined with heightened sensitivity when even the slightest amount of criticism is directed at him or her.

Thus, while narcissism in popular culture is often used as a pejorative term and an insult aimed at people like actors, models, and other celebrities who display high degrees of self-love and satisfaction, NPD is actually a psychological term that is quite distinct from merely having high self-esteem. The key to understanding this aspect of dark psychology is that the narcissist's image of himself or herself is often completely and entirely idealized, grandiose, and inflated and cannot be justified with any factual, meaningful accomplishments or capacities that may make such claims believable. As a result of this discord between expectation and reality, the demanding, manipulative, inconsiderate, self-centered, and arrogant behavior of the narcissist can cause problems not only for himself or herself, but for all of the people in his or her life.

# 2. Machiavellianism

Strictly defined, Machiavellianism is the political philosophy of Niccolò Machiavelli, who lived from 1469 until 1527 in Italy. In contemporary society, Machiavellianism is a term used to describe the popular understanding of people who are perceived as displaying very high political or professional ambitions. In psychology, however, the Machiavellianism scale is used to measure the degree to which people with deviant personalities display manipulative behavior.

Machiavelli wrote The Prince, a political treatise in which he stated that sincerity, honesty, and other virtues were certainly admirable qualities, but that in politics, the capacity to engage in deceit, treachery, and other forms of criminal behavior were acceptable if there were no other means of achieving political aims to protect one's interests.

Popular misconceptions reduce this entire philosophy to the view that "the end justifies the means." To be fair, Machiavelli himself insisted that the more important part of this equation was ensuring that the end itself must first be justified. Furthermore, it is better to achieve such ends using means devoid of treachery whenever possible because there is less risk to the interests of the actor.

Thus, seeking the most effective means of achieving a political end may not necessarily lead to the most treacherous. In addition, not all political ends that have been justified as worth pursuing must be pursued. In many cases, the mere threat that a certain course of action may be pursued may be enough to achieve that end. In some cases, the treachery may be as mild as making a credible threat to take action that is not really even intended.

In contemporary society, many people overlook the fact that Machiavellianism is part of the "Dark Triad" of dark psychology and tacitly approve of the deviant behavior of political and business leaders who are able to amass great power or wealth. However, as a psychological disorder, Machiavellianism is entirely different from a chosen path to political power.

The person displaying Machiavellian personality traits does not consider whether his or her actions are the most effective means to achieving his or her goals, whether there are alternatives that do not involve deceit or treachery, or even whether the ultimate result of his or her actions is worth achieving. The Machiavellian personality is not evidence of a strategic or calculating mind attempting to achieve a worthwhile objective in a contentious environment. Instead, it is always on, whether the situation calls for a cold, calculating, and manipulative approach or not.

For example, we have all called in sick to work when we really just wanted a day off. But for most of us, such conduct is not how we behave normally, and after such acts of dishonesty, many of us feel guilty. Those who display a high degree of Machiavellianism would not just lie when they want a day off; they see lying and dishonesty as the only way to conduct themselves in all situations, regardless of whether doing so results in any benefit.

What's more, because of the degree of social acceptance and tacit approval granted to Machiavellian personalities who successfully attain political power, their presence in society does not receive the kind of negative attention accorded to the other two members of the Dark Triad—psychopathy and narcissism.

# 3. Psychopathy

Psychopathy is defined as a mental disorder with several identifying characteristics that include antisocial behavior, amorality, an inability to develop empathy or to establish meaningful personal relationships, extreme egocentricity, and recidivism, with repeated violations resulting from an apparent inability to learn from the consequences of earlier transgressions. Antisocial behavior, in turn, is defined as behavior based upon a goal of violating formal and/or informal rules of social conduct through criminal activity or through acts of personal, private protest, or opposition, all of which is directed against other individuals or society in general.

Egocentricity is behavior is when the offending person sees himself or herself as the central focus of the world, or at least of all dominant social and political activity. Empathy is the ability to view and understand events, thoughts, emotions, and beliefs from the perspective of others, and is considered one of the most important psychological components for establishing successful, ongoing relationships.

Amorality is entirely different from immorality. An immoral act is an act which violates established moral codes. A person who is immoral can be confronted with his or her actions with the expectation that he or she will recognize that his or her actions are offensive form a moral, if not a legal, standpoint. Amorality, on the other hand, represents a psychology that does not recognize that any moral codes exist, or if they do, that they have no value in determining whether or not to act in one way or another.

Thus, someone displaying psychopathy may commit horrendous acts that cause tremendous psychological and physical trauma and not ever understand that what he or she has done is wrong. Worse still, those who display signs of psychopathy usually worsen over time because they are unable to make the connection between the problems in their lives and in the lives of those in the world around them and their own harmful and destructive actions.

# The Dark Triad in Practive

The professional workplace has acknowledged the presence of people exhibiting Dark Triad characteristics.

The following diagram illustrates that they are tolerated for their efficiency and their ability to get things done but contrasts that ability with the negative effects it has on their ability to form personal relationships:

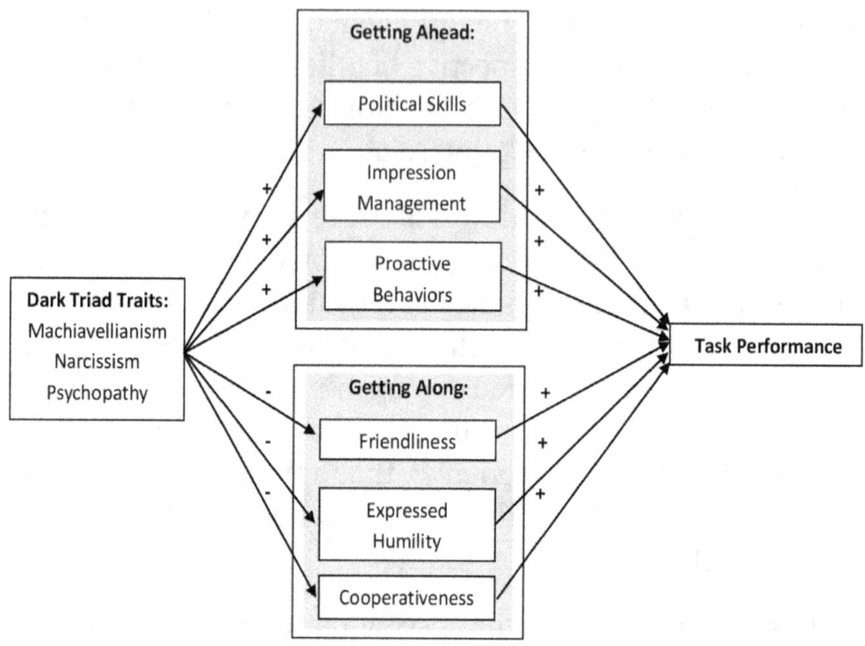


*(Benjamin McLarty, Mississippi State University, 2015)*

The remainder will discuss a wide variety of people and situations in which you may find one, two, all three, or some combination of these Dark Triad personalities working in concert around you.

The clinical descriptions are easy enough to categorize, and in isolation, it can be fairly straightforward to separate one type of dark psychology from another. The real world is a lot messier. Many of us have grown accustomed to so-called "toxic relationships," whether they are relationships with our partners, our co-workers, our family members, our bosses, or our political and community leaders.

In addition, manifestations of dark psychology are often far more mundane than the dramatic examples we see in major television and film productions about the romantic lives of serial killers and other criminals. The more we accept these relationships as normal, the more difficult it will be to identify them as problematic.

Remember that psychological, emotional, and social predators do not think of themselves as sick. Their lack of morality and empathy, and their adaption from a very early age to live according to rules and methods you may find horribly wrong, can make their presence intimidating. However, you should also remember that even when their amorality and lack of empathy may allow them to enjoy an unjust advantage in relationships, their mental capacities are the result of underdevelopment, not a higher evolutionary state.

# CHAPTER 3

# Another
# Dark Personalities

MORAL DISENGAGEMENT IS A TERM RELATED to social psychology. It is the act of convincing your own mind that ethical and moral standards don't apply to you. A person suffering from moral disengagement is able to disconnect the part of the brain that tells them what they are doing is wrong. They often are part of inhumane activities to which they justify through verbally recited morals, comparison to others, removing responsibility from themselves, shrugging of serious injuries to others as if they weren't as bad as they seemed, and one of the worst, they immediately begin to dehumanize the person in which they have acted against.

One not so talked about form of moral disengagement is used in military tactic on a daily basis. The military morally justifies the killing of "enemies" for the greater good of society. They go so far as to convince the soldiers that their actions made them heroes. And this does not just happen to the members of the military, but to society as well when we shake the hand of a soldier and justify the actions they took because we've been told that there is some sort of moral caveat when it comes to enemy lives.

# The Disengaged Morally Personalities

## 1. Egoism

Psychological egoism within a personality creates a belief that every motive you have is for the betterment of yourself. Egoists are often considered nonmoral and do not all operate in the same fashion. There is no specific, verifiable course or personality that an egoist takes but the base of their person cares for themselves first over all others.

Now that we understand some of the major traits within Dark Psychology, we will be able to better pinpoint why the following four are more often diagnosed on a clinical level. They can arguably also be some of the worst Dark Personality traits you could have.

## 2. Sadism

Sadism can also be manifested in sex. It is referred to as psychosexual disorder. An individual with this kind of a disorder finds gratification out of inflicting pain to their partner during sex. Other individuals find sexual gratification when pain is inflicted upon them. Most sadists, however, prefer a sexual partner that is not masochistic so that they enjoy inflicting pain on them or the unwillingness of the victim to engage in sadistic sexual pleasure.

There are various levels of violence during sex. Some are mild with some being so severe that they result in injuries. The sadist may find satisfaction, not on the actual pain they inflict on their victim but rather from the mental torture of the victim. Sadism has also been associated with violent crimes such as murder or rape.

Individuals that are purposely cruel to others for pleasure are also described as sadistic. They derive pleasure out of domineering and humiliating their victims even in social settings. Others may use sarcasm as a form to publicly humiliate their victims and feel good about it.

# 3. Selfishness

Self-interest is pretty simple to explain in normal terms. It is simply putting yourself before all others despite the cost to the other party. In psychology, there are two subsets of self-interest, egoism and narcissism which will be explained below. Within the philosophical realm of self-interest, there are several concepts behind self-interest.

- Enlightened Self-Interest - This concept states that if you do for others, ultimately you will be serving your own self-interest as well.

- Ethical Egoism - This concept is the thought that people should do what is best for themselves.

- Rational Egoism - This belief centers around the idea that any rational action that you take should always be done in your own self-interest.

- Hedonism - Hedonism makes the assertion that the only type of good is pleasure. Hedonism also includes the pre-Socratic Cyrenaic and the philosophical system known as Epicureanism.

- Individualism - This is a philosophy that teaches people to have a very strong sense of self-worth.

# 4. Spitefulness

Spitefulness dates back to even before human beings existed. In fact, spite has been studied within organisms in order to further understand the relevance in the human species. In the land of ash and fire, when the Earth was transitioning into a greener and more livable space, organisms were forming deep in the watery depths of the oceans. Some of these organisms had a reactionary defense that released toxins that killed the other organisms. In doing so, however, those same toxins often killed the releaser. Ever heard the saying, "cut off your nose to spite your face?"

# The Role to Use and Defense

There are various people that use dark psychology as well as manipulation tactics to get what they want. Some of these people are:

- Narcissists – Narcissistic people that are described as having narcissistic personality disorders have a bloated ego and an inflated sense of importance. They need others to validate that they are more superior. They want to be worshiped, adored and held in high esteem. They often make use of dark psychology tactics to get what they want. Some of the tactics they use include unethical persuasion as well as manipulations.

- Sociopaths – Individuals that sociopathic disorder disorders are intelligent, charming, and in some cases impulsive. They lack the ability to have an emotional connection to others. They use dark psychology tactics to create a superficial relationship while taking advantage of others.

- Attorneys – Most attorneys are driven by winning a case. As a result, they use dark persuasion tactics so that they influence the outcome.

- Politicians – In order to convince people to trust them and vote for them, politicians are known to use dark psychology tactics of persuasion to get their way.

- Salespeople – Most salespeople work on targets. They are focused on closing a sale that they use dark tactics as a way to motivate and persuade a person to buy what they are selling.

- Leaders – To get their subordinates to perform higher or put more effort into their work, some leaders resort in using dark tactics as a motivation or persuasion tool.

- Public speakers – Speakers understand the importance of heightening the emotional state of their audience. They know by doing this, they can sell more products or services and so they use dark tactics to persuade their audience.

- Selfish people – Anyone can be selfish. If you have an agenda to benefit at the expense of others then you are selfish. To achieve one's agenda, an individual may result in using dark tactics to convince others in order to meet their selfish needs.

As an individual, it is important to differentiate between using dark tactics of motivation and persuasion and ethical tactics. You must ask yourself the intent of your persuasion. Is it to benefit self only or does it benefit others? If the intent is only for your benefit, it can easily fall under dark psychology tactics.

You should always aim at having a mutually benefiting outcome and believe that is what you are doing. To know if your tactics are falling more on the dark side of the ethical side, you need to ask yourself the following:

- What is your goal in the interaction and who stands to gain from it?

- Do you feel good at your approach in the interaction?

- Are you being completely honest and open in your interactions?

- Will the interaction result in a long-term benefit for both parties?

- Will the tactics use the result in a trusting relationship with the other person?

- To be successful in your relationships, work, parenting or leadership, you must assess yourself and determine if your tactics to motivate and persuade are ethical or selfish.

# Dark Psychology Key Points

- Dark psychology is the study of the dark side of human personality. This kind of study provides a sharp contrast to the popular study of positive personality traits.

- Dark psychology, as a study, seeks to understand the feelings, perceptions, and thoughts of these people, as well as how the subjective processing systems possessed by these individuals work antithetically to what is considered a contemporary understanding of human behavior.

- Dark singularity: according to dark psychology, there is a region in the human psyche that enables the commission of atrocious acts without purpose among some humans. This is what is commonly referred to as dark singularity.

- Dark continuum: again, according to dark psychology, as humans, we have a reservoir of malicious intent towards one another and the acts we may want to commit in this case range from minimally intrusive acts to outright hideous psychotic and deviant behaviors for which we may not have cohesive rationality.

- Dark factor: there are factors that may act as accelerants that are considered when approaching dark singularity. When these accelerants are mitigated and where the heinous nature of a person is on the dark continuum, then it is referred to as the dark continuum.

- Dark triad: in dark psychology, the dark triad consists of the personality traits of narcissism, psychopathy, and Machiavellianism. They possess malevolent qualities, as described above.

- Characteristics of People with Negative Personality Traits - These types of individuals are not the ordinary types, and oftentimes, they have a tendency to confuse even psychologists—thanks to their high scores on measures of callousness—which is described as the lack of empathy for others.

## EXERCISE:

Short dark triad, test to measure of the "dark triad" of personality.

https://openpsychometrics.org/tests/SD3/

# CHAPTER 4

# Behavioral Traits of Favorite Victims of Manipulators Emotional

**P**OWER IS A COMPONENT OF MANIPULATION, but not the only component. Intelligent and sensitive people have power, but they do not use it to manipulate others.

## Sensitive people

The person who does the manipulation is the one that has greater comparative power and is unable to get what he wants in mutual agreement or thought other means and rests to underhanded tactic which usually results in manipulation.

To neutralize the emotional manipulation, you have to stop caring what the other person says or feels. This balances the power they have over you. Power to compel action using external force is not emotional manipulation – and if you believe that physical harm may result from denial of request by the aggressor then you have a problem greater than emotional manipulation and beyond the scope of the topic. But the power to compel you from within you is emotional manipulation.

That gives you two alternatives. The first it can either weaken you out, or it can make you realize that you have the ultimate power over what goes on inside. Don't let anyone on the outside to dictate what goes on inside.

Ultimately only you have the power of your own destiny and you need to make it a habit to remember that.

# Empathic people

An empath is someone who absorbs more emotion that a typical person. If they can sense tremendously more than anyone else then the slighted detection that the other person would like you to do something for them will be magnified and they would go about doing it just so as to not feel bad about it. This does not mean the other person has the power over the empath.

It is more prevalent that women are more empathic and the softer side of the equation. Nothing wrong with that, but when you remind someone that that is who they are, they take on the stereotypes and then they become easier to manipulate.

Being told that you are beautiful, sexy, gorgeous are all ways that lead to a certain form of weakening of your intellect and those results in the path to manipulation. Well, not all times but it can be. Men tend to pay obsequious compliments to women so that they can take advantage of the situation. It is not the complement that breaks them, but the reminder that they are women in conjunction with the complement.

Your frame of mind needs to be strengthened before the event. It's like building the walls to a medieval city. You don't erect the walls just when the marauding armies arrive you build them ahead of time.

The other thing that you have to do is alter the stereotype that you have of your gender and yourself. Once you neutralize that, it's harder for anyone to use that to get you to submit. If you look at the art of enslaving people, even till today, a few slave owners can control hundreds of slaves. Why? Can't the slaves overpower them with numbers? No, because their frame of mind has been manipulated and their mind has submitted,

Protect your mind and your thoughts and you will be able to fend off a large part of the manipulating aggressor.

# Fear of loneliness

A victim who seems lonely, seeking support, comfort, and desperate is more likely to be love bombed and at a higher intensity than others. If the victim is more grounded, then they will need a less intense, and maybe more subtle, way in the love bombing.

The idea behind working with love bombing is that it is going to create an intense feeling of affection, trust, and compliance from the victim over to their manipulator. The extent of which love bombing is going to be used, and the person it is used on, will often depend on how the manipulator assesses the situation.

# Fear of disappointing others

If your insecurities are triggering you to believe negative thoughts, which will materialize into unfavorable activities, that's when your partnership can begin feeling several of the adverse effects of your insecurity. It might not take place overnight yet understand that it's OK if you require to overcome some insecurities, whether that's on your very own, with a therapist, or with the love and support of your companion. Below are seven signs that your instabilities are influencing your connection, according to professionals.

Instability comes from our concern of 'not having sufficient' or 'not being enough'. These anxieties are vanity based. When we are unconfident, we bother with what others think about us and also do not have a strong feeling of self and even healthy self-worth. Here are a couple of indications of instability that can indicate you need to lock out the voice of the ego and be true to on your own.

# 1. Flaunting

One of the most usual indicators of instability is boasting regarding what you have and what you have attained. Troubled individuals possess of trying to thrill other individuals.

They then end up being hopeless for recognition from the world exterior. Nonetheless, if you have a protected sense of self, you don't feel the requirement to excite others regularly. As well as you certainly do not need other people to validate you.

# 2. Regulating

Individuals who are monitoring can occasionally appear to be stable. Nevertheless, controlling behavior originates from anxiety and also insecurity. It is just one of the most common indications of instability. When we are afraid that we may not be able to deal with what life tosses at us, we attempt frantically to regulate the globe around us as well as maintain it within appropriate boundaries so that we feel risk-free and safe and secure. This can lead us to control other people as we can just feel safe if they act in foreseeable ways. When we understand that we can handle life, whatever happens, we no more feel the demand to regulate every little thing to feel secure rigidly. We can, after that, start to go with the flow and delight in life in all its messy glory.

# 3. Stress and anxiety

Anxiety often originates from a sensation of not being good enough, as well. Frequently when we are anxious, we are afraid of what other people may think of us, or we are so scared we will ruin in some way. Individuals that are protected in themselves don't feel anxious about points a lot. This is since they do not put so much emphasis on being right regularly. Although they might still establish high requirements for themselves, they do not defeat themselves up for every regarded mistake. They approve that they are only human, which often they will undoubtedly obtain things wrong and that's okay.

# 4. Individuals pleasing

A clear sign of instability is the demand to please other individuals at all times. This hinders of living your very own life. It can occasionally seem like your life does not belong to you when you are regularly attempting to make others happy. People with high self-esteem show caring and empathy for others but do not feel they are accountable for another individuals' happiness. And that is real. You are exempt for another individuals' satisfaction, and you do not require to secure or rescue them from every unpleasant thing they might experience.

If you are a people pleaser, you must make room in your life for you. You must obtain a possibility to do the things that make you happy and follow your very own desires and also not merely assist others in accomplishing theirs. However, people-pleasing can result in bitterness and even a feeling of martyrdom. This is not a healthy and balanced method to be. People-pleasing is terrible for you as well as it is likewise bad for others as it is often harmful to their growth, too.

# 5. Perfectionism

If you seem like nothing you do is good enough, or you spend an excessive amount of time obtaining points 'perfect,' then this may signify insecurity. This typically boils down to a fear of failure or criticism. You find it tough to allow go and proceed from a job since you fear the outcome may not be what you hoped. Regrettably, this can result in you obtaining stuck, never being able to finish things or investing much too lengthy on whatever you do. This can suggest you stop working to meet due dates or let people down. This harms your self-esteem and also can be a descending spiral. Perfectionism can be tough to escape from, but once again, having a healthy and balanced feeling of self, as well as being kinder and also more accepting of that you are, is the place to start.

# 6. Anxiety

Feelings of anxiety can often signify insecurity. Clinical depression can happen when a buildup of tension triggers you to pull back from life. Stress commonly makes us take out of the world to ensure that we won't get injured or criticized or won't fall short. By developing a strong feeling of self, you can venture out right into the world without a lot of anxiety and also anxiety. Of course, stress is not always straightforward to recoup from, however, beginning with small acts of self-care and being mild with on your own is an excellent way to start to move out of crippling clinical depression.

# CHAPTER 5.

# Dependent Personality Disorders and Emotional Dependency

Individuals with dependent personality disorder are afraid of separating or being left by significant people in their lives, which can cause needy behavior. This behavior can leave the individual at risk of being used by others.

## Dependent Personality Disorders

As individuals with dependent personality disorder need continuous support, they may struggle to make decisions or to finish projects on their own. They often put themselves down and avoid disagreeing with others even when they know the person is incorrect.

Dependent personality disorder is a pervasive fear that results in clinging behavior in early adulthood, whereby those affected have difficulty making normal decisions throughout their daily lives without constant and excessive reassurance from others and advice from others (American Psychiatric Association, 2013). Anxiety and depression are key symptoms associated with this disorder, which manifest in everyday life.

Dependent personality disorder often brings with its feelings of self-doubt and pessimism, both of which belittle the assets and abilities of the individual. Disapproval or criticism is taken as proof of being worthless, which is why many people will seek dominance and overprotection from other people. In return, the individual will become dependent and submissive, out of fear that they cannot live without help from others.

An individual with dependent personality disorder will face difficulty making everyday decisions, will need other people to take responsibility for the major areas of their life, will not express disagreement with others, and will not start projects or do things on their own. Individuals will also feel uncomfortable if they are left alone and will go to great lengths to get the support they need from others. They remain unrealistically preoccupied with the fear of having to take care of themselves.

Given that such disorders revolve around long-term behavioral patterns, most personality disorders, including dependent personality disorder, are diagnosed in adulthood.

Those who suffer from dependent personality disorder often deal with secondary symptoms, which include depression, anxiety, and difficulties adjusting to life changes.

Studies indicate that there is a prevalence of between 0.4 and 1.5% of dependent personality disorder in the general population (Grant et al., 2004). Many of those with this disorder experience few symptoms as a child, but the severity of the symptoms increases with age and can last into their 40s and 50s.

How do you know if you have developed emotional dependency/codependency in a relationship?

# Needy

A codependent partner is insecure with low self-esteem. These individuals tend to be clingy and emotionally unstable. Your actions will never be enough to convince your partner that you value them as "enough." They will overanalyze your actions in an effort to decipher what you're actually saying, nothing will be taken at face value. These partners will need constant validation that they are needed and cared for.

# Indecisive

Codependent partners will always place the interests of others above their own. Mistrust of their own judgment will also be present. These factors together can mean that your codependent partner does not feel comfortable making any decisions on their own. These behaviors will give an impression of flakiness.

# Controlling

These partners may believe that they have your best interests at heart. This can lead to controlling behavior that would be easy to confuse for narcissism. Emotional manipulation will be used to encourage their partner in the direction that better serves the needs of the codependent.

Codependent partners are well versed in guilt and shame. These two emotions will be used to steer the actions of those around them. Denial will keep the codependent partner from understanding that they are intentionally guiding the actions of others.

Codependent manipulation is more gentle than narcissistic manipulation. The resentful codependent partner will use their own tears or sadness to steer their partners in the direction that they want them to go. They will slam doors and make passive-aggressive remarks to show that they are angry, but they will not explain why they are upset.

# Enjoying the Misery

Codependent partners (like narcissists) unintentionally relish the role of the victim. This title can be used to grant them both control and pity. This behavior also means that any codependent that wanders into a relationship with a narcissist is going to stay there. Abuse is not enjoyable, but the codependent will accept it in order to further nail down the title of "victim."

Narcissists are professional takers, and codependents are professional givers. The two sides become entrenched in a relationship that exploits the weaknesses of one partner and caters to the manipulative nature of the other. If you suspect that you might be codependent, then you must seek therapy. You must take action to change this behavior or you will seek out abusive partners over and over again.

Codependent partners in normal relationships have trouble accepting that they are worthy of basic respect and affection. When these individuals are placed with a narcissist, the abuser affirms the fear that they aren't good enough.

The codependent is unhappy, but they also believe that they are deserving of the abuse they receive. These two disorders were created from the same place will forever be bound together.

# Secret Rules

Codependent partners are unwilling to share their wants and needs with their partners. They view themselves as being undeserving of having these needs met. They will create expectations within their own mind, and then be bitter when their partner behaves in opposition to their rules. At no point in time have they communicated their boundaries; the partner is meant to guess.

Codependents and narcissists both have an inability to see the others as being disconnected from themselves. Everyone else is believed to think in the same way that they do. Codependents will assume that partners have the same boundaries that they do. They will assume that romantic behavior is defined in the same way for both them and their partner. They will react in sadness when their partner fails to behave in the way that they behave to assert the other person's value.

## EXERCISE:

HOW MUCH DO YOU KNOW YOURSELF?

This test will help you analyze your habits and attitudes to get to know you better. Answer questions without thinking too much, give the first answer that comes to mind and find out how much you know yourself.

1. If it served my purposes, I wouldn't hesitate to lie to a doorman or a vigilante.
2. I would never cut in front of someone in line.
3. If I could sneak into a movie theater without being discovered, I would most likely do it.
4. I happened to get revenge on those who offended me.
5. If a waiter forgot to take my order, I'd pretend nothing happened.
6. I would never allow anyone else to be reprimanded for my mistakes.
7. If I don't know something, I have no trouble admitting it.
8. I try to be honest in any situation.
9. I think I'm less biased than most people.
10. My manners at the table are impeccable both at home and in restaurants.

CALCULATE THE SCORE:

To calculate your score, assign 1 point for each response equal to yours.

1. False  2. True  3. False  4. False  5. False  6. True  7. True  8. True  9. True  10. True

0 to 4 points: the opinion that others have of you interests you relatively. Socially you don't like to even out and you like to show yourself different and independent. Often you are too forgiving with yourself and if you were to be excluded from a group you would not lose sleep.

5 to 8 points: you're interested in being accepted by others, but it's certainly not your priority. You always show yourself how you are with your merits and your flaws.

9 to 10 points: you want to be accepted at all costs. Maybe you're looking for the approval of others more than you should. You're pretty shy if it's about saying yours and you feel inferior.

# CHAPTER 6

# How to Strengthen Yourself

TAKE RESPONSIBILITY FOR YOUR ACTIONS. Even if you are realizing now that you have or are being manipulated, don't wallow in regret. Don't feel sorry or bad about yourself. Realize that everyone has been manipulated at least once in their lives. The important thing is that you realize it now and can now take the step toward shedding the role of the victim. When you remain in the victim mentality – thinking that you are "so dumb" for letting someone manipulate you or that you will only repeat these mistakes – you remain an easy target.

Stepping out of the victim role and into the role of the manipulator is your first step in solidifying your identity and steeling yourself mentally. Own up to how you have been used in the past and move on from it. Just because it happened once or twice or three or even hundreds of times does not mean that it has to keep happening. Start thinking of yourself as a manipulator every day. Distance yourself from victim thinking and take control. Look at yourself in the mirror every day and say to your reflection "I am in control." It may feel silly at first, but it is an effective way to program yourself out of victim thinking.

Developing a strong mentality will make it much easier for you to impose your influence on someone else and keep other people from doing the same to you. It is what you must do if you want to become a skilled manipulator. Learning the techniques is not enough. Manipulation is a mental exercise and keeping a strong mind will make you more successful at this exercise. Stepping out of the victim role is just the first step. There is more you can do to fortify your mind and identity.

# Meditation and Grounding

A strong mind is a grounded mind, but what does it mean to be mentally grounded? Being mentally grounded means that you have an unwavering point of reference to who you are at your core. Think of it like your own mental refuge to turn to when life gets too chaotic. In terms of manipulation, being mentally grounded will help center you from the lies that you may have to tell or the lies that you hear. It was stated earlier that when practicing manipulation, it can be very easy to get lost or out of touch with your own reality.

That is where mental grounding comes into play. When you are mentally grounded you will never lose touch with your own reality and lose yourself in the many roles you may have to play when manipulating. It isn't always easy to find mental grounding though and it can be even more difficult to maintain. Before we get into ways you can become more mentally grounded, be aware that this is not a one-and-done practice. However, you find best to mentally ground your-self should become a regular if not every day routine for you. Think of your mind like a car. When you manipulate, or even when you are just out in the world and interacting with others, you are putting miles on your mind. Every once in a while, you need to change the oil and tune it up. For as long as you have a brain, you need to practice regular mental grounding.

So, let's look at some ways to achieve a grounded mind:

- **Meditation** – Meditation is the practice of clearing your mind and focusing on your breathing. This is very difficult to do at first but the more you prac-tice it, the better you will get at it and the more you will benefit from it. Try finding a quiet little spot where you can sit down on the ground or lay. This should be somewhere you will not be disturbed. Start with just 20 minutes a day in which you come to rest in this place, close your eyes, try to clear your mind and focus only on your breathing pattern. Focus solely on maintain-ing a uniform breathing pattern. When you feel more comfortable doing this for 20 minutes, increase it to ten more minutes and on and on in that fashion.

- **Being Amongst Nature** – There is a Bud-dhist parable called "The Sermon of the Inanimate." In this parable, a practitioner sat quietly in a forest and ob-served the nature around him; the trees, the grass, the rocks etc.

He found that inanimate nature, by merit of being still has a lot to teach us. Being amongst nature is a good way to find your mental grounding. It doesn't have to be a forest. It could be a small park in your neighborhood. Just as long as you are more or less surrounded by natural things. Spend time here regularly and you will come to find that the needs and concerns of society are not the same as the needs and concerns of nature. The trees are not stressed about work. The rocks don't care about material matters like cars and clothes. Unfortunately, we cannot be in this state of bare tranquility all the time but finding your own nature refuge can go a long way towards re-centering and refocusing on what is important and real in your life.

- **Take Night Walks** – Have you ever noticed that when you walk you think a bit clearer? Maybe you have taken a walk with someone and found that you have more to talk about while walking. There is a reason for that. When our bodies are active our blood is flowing more which means more blood flow to the brain. Try taking a walk at night when you know there won't be a lot of cars or other people on the street. Think about your day and your interactions. Evaluate them beyond the surface encounters and compare them to what you believe and feel. This just might help you get to the hearts of various matters better and realize where your grounding lies.

# Practice Improving Your Frame Control

Mental grounding helps a lot in maintaining your frame because your frame is what you truly believe to be true and what you care about in life. You cannot maintain your frame without first finding your mental grounding. That is why it is important to practice grounding as often as possible. When you constantly remind yourself of your beliefs it will be that much easier to maintain your frame.

A strong frame is all about not wavering under criticism and pressure. You will be challenged a lot, especially when you are using any of the tactics you have learned here. Under this pressure you must be confident that what you believe is right and true. You can use any of the tips we have talked about for increasing charisma and confidence like standing/sitting up straight, speaking deliberately and maintaining intent eye-contact. Increasing your level of confidence will help you build a song self-frame.

Use these techniques and practices with patience, perseverance, care and awareness. Remember always that having a strong mind is the first step toward being able to sway anybody. Know that the only way to protect yourself from other manipulators is to have a strong mind. Keep in touch with your sense of self at all times. If you do all of these things and take to heart all of the techniques and tactics that you have learned here, you will find your definition of success in psychological wisdom and understanding.

The goal here is to keep you out on the lookout for the dark manipulators who may show up in your life. When you know some of the signs to watch out for, and you understand dark psychology, you can protect yourself and stay safe! You are the one who should be in control of your own mind. Don't let someone else take that away from you!

## EXERCISE:

https://mindfulnessexercises.com/50-free-mindfulness-meditations/

# CHAPTER 7

# What is Emotional Manipulation?

T HERE ARE SEVERAL TYPES OF EMOTIONAL MANIPULATION because it can often depend on where the manipulator is or who they are manipulating. For example, there are some manipulators who focus on workplace tactics while others will manipulate their significant other. Of course, there are manipulators who will use their tactics no matter where they are or who they are with.

## Categories of Emotionally Manipulative

According to psychology professor George K. Simon, effective psychological manipulation mainly involves the manipulator with the following intent and actions:

- Hiding and being affable to hostile activities and behaviors

- Understanding the victim's psychological weaknesses to assess which tactics would probably be the most successful

- Having a sufficient level of ruthlessness to allow no misgivings about harming the victim if needed

Consequently, the abuse is likely to be done through covert violent means.

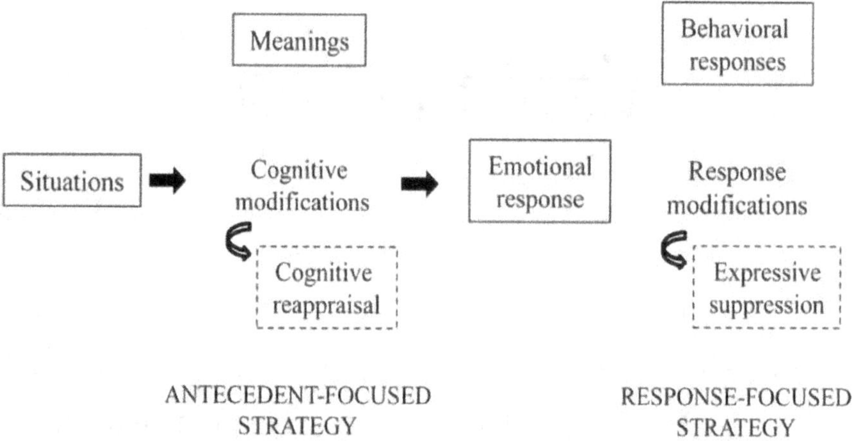


# Emotional Manipulation in Relationships

Long haul control can have genuine impacts in cozy connections, including those between companions, relatives, and sentimental accomplices. Control can decay the strength of a relationship and lead to the poor psychological well-being of those in the relationship or even the disintegration of the relationship.

In a marriage or association, control can make one accomplice feel harassed, segregated, or useless.

Indeed, even in solid connections, one accomplice may coincidentally control the other so as to evade showdown or even trying to shield their accomplice from inclination loaded. Numerous individuals may even realize they are being controlled in their relationship and neglect or make light of it. Control in personal connections can take numerous structures, including embellishment, blame, blessing giving or specifically indicating warmth, mystery keeping, and latent hostility.

Guardians who control their kids may set their kids up for blame, wretchedness, uneasiness, eating issues, and other emotional wellness conditions. One investigation likewise uncovered that guardians who normally use control strategies on their kids may improve the probability their youngsters will likewise utilize manipulative conduct. Indications of control in the parent-youngster relationship may incorporate making the tyke feel regretful, absence of responsibility from a parent, minimizing a tyke's accomplishments, and a should be associated with numerous parts of the kid's life.

# Emotional Manipulations in Friendships

Individuals may likewise feel controlled in the event that they are a piece of a kinship that has turned out to be harmful. In manipulative fellowships, one individual might utilize the other to address their very own issues to the detriment of their friend's. A manipulative companion may utilize blame or intimidation to concentrate favors, for example, crediting cash, or they may possibly contact that companion when they need their very own passionate needs met and may discover pardons when their companion has needs in the relationship.

# Emotional Manipulation at Work

Many people deal with workplace manipulation at some point in their career. Sometimes it is because one of their co-workers is a manipulator while other times it is everyday forms of manipulation. For example, a co-worker manipulates you into helping them with their task or gets you to do their task. They only do this because they don't like this specific responsibility.

Sometimes you will start to notice your supervisor is a manipulator. Unfortunately, this is highly common in the workplace as many supervisors have used manipulation to get their position, especially if they worked themselves up the ladder. However, you should never assume your supervisor is manipulative. If they are, they will typically demonstrate signs of being a manipulator, such as bullying, blaming others, guilting their staff, giving staff the silent treatment, and distorting facts.

One way you know if you work with a manipulator is by the way you are treated. Manipulators need to make sure you know your place, meaning you are beneath them. Therefore, they will often make sarcastic comments that make you feel inferior. For example, you come to work one day in professional attire that is more casual than your company usually wears. Instead of a white shirt and a suit, you are wearing a white shirt with slacks. When your co-worker notices your attire, they start to belittle your clothes, making fun of your lower-paying income and that you can't afford nicer clothes.

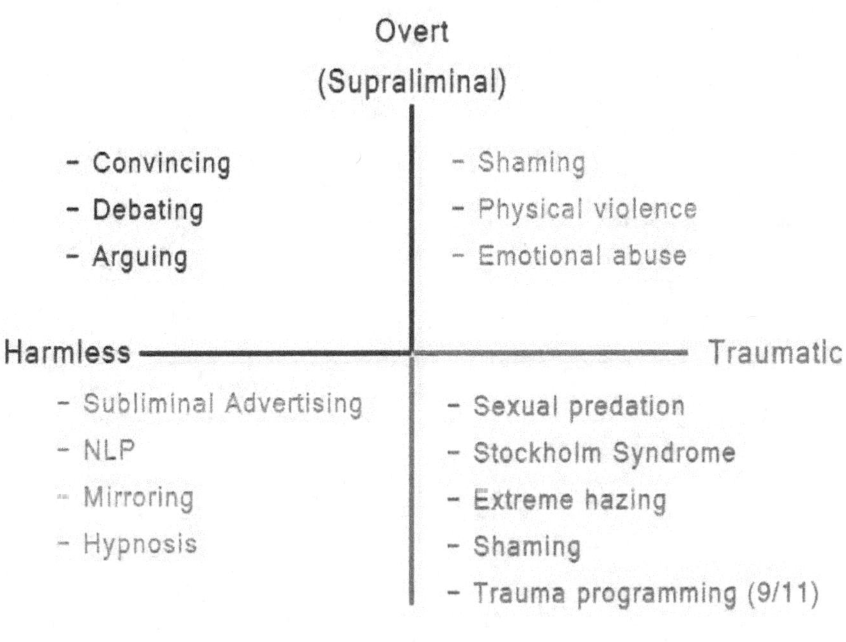

Overt
(Supraliminal)
- Convincing
- Debating
- Arguing
- Shaming
- Physical violence
- Emotional abuse
Harmless
Traumatic
- Subliminal Advertising
- NLP
- Mirroring
- Hypnosis
- Sexual predation
- Stockholm Syndrome
- Extreme hazing
- Shaming
- Trauma programming (9/11)
Covert
(Subliminal)

# CHAPTER 8

# What is Covert Emotional Manipulation?

COVERT EMOTIONAL MANIPULATION is a part of any form of manipulation. However, it is stronger in people who are known as "master manipulators" or people who will manipulate anyone in order to get anything they want. It is not as strong in manipulation tactics people use when they tell someone they are fine, even though something is wrong.

At the base of manipulation is working to change the way people feel and think, which is covert emotional manipulation. They focus on your conscious awareness in order to control you. Because of this, people don't often realize that they are being manipulated.

First, the manipulator will get you to trust them. Then, they will start to control the way you feel, think, and perceive situations. This will happen slowly as they don't want you to catch on to the manipulation. Once they feel that your emotions and thoughts are in their hands, they will start to tear apart your confidence.

A master manipulator knows they have to lower your self-esteem in order to control you the way they want to. They will also work to take away your identity, which allows you to fully become theirs.

While they are trying to break you down emotionally and mentally, they will also try to keep you away from your family and friends. One of the biggest reasons for this is people who knew you before they came into your life are a threat to them. Your family and friends will notice a change in you, and they won't like it. They will try to find out why you are changing and, typically very quickly, they point their fingers at the manipulator.

When this happens, your friends and family will do what they can to try to see what this person is doing to you and how you are being treated. This is one of the most common signs of manipulation in relationships.

Of course, you will start to notice a change within yourself. Unfortunately, it is usually after the manipulator has had control over you. You start to notice yourself change when you begin to feel different. You might notice you have anxiety, you are depressed, having trouble sleeping, you struggle trusting people you once trusted, and you have become increasingly isolated ("About Covert Emotional Manipulation", n.d.).

For most people, it is hard to spot the signs of manipulators. This is especially true for people who suffer from manipulation from their significant other. In general, it is hard to spot certain signs of manipulation. Furthermore, it is often harder to spot these behaviors from people who you love and believe love you back.

In relationships, people often turn a "blind eye" to their significant other's manipulative ways because they see them as faults. We work to understand the faults of each other in relationships.

# What is the Manipulator's Thing to Do?

You may wonder; what are manipulators trying to do? Why do they put so much work into manipulating others, instead of just focusing on improving themselves?

The fact is that manipulators have a deep-seated psychological need to control others, so they seek to "weaken" their victims in order to gain dominance over them. When they manipulate others, they are trying to cancel their willpower, to destroy their self-esteem, to seek passive-aggressive revenge against them, or to confuse their reality so that they become more malleable.

Let's look at how and why manipulators do those four things.

# CHAPTER 9

# Cancellation of Willpower

IT'S BECAUSE OF OUR WILLPOWER that we are able to retain control over our lives and to resist people's attempts to dominate us and force us to do their bidding. That is why one of the primary intentions of manipulative people is to obliterate our willpower.

So, how can someone take away your willpower? Well, first, you have to understand that willpower isn't unlimited. We can lose our will power through a process that psychologists refer to as "ego depletion." To understand this, you have to think of willpower as a resource that may be renewable, but it can only be renewed at a slow pace. So, if we spend that resource on one thing, we have less of it to spend on another thing that demands it. So, ego depletion is the outcome that occurs when we spend all the willpower that we have, and we are left without adequate willpower in the face of subsequent challenges.

Manipulative people know that willpower doesn't come from a bottomless pit, so they tend to overload us with scenarios where we are forced to use our willpower until that willpower gets depleted. For example, a malicious person may keep trying to agitate you, while you keep trying to stay calm and keep your cool. However, if he keeps doing it for a prolonged period of time, chances are you will get to a point where you snap and react with anger.

Psychologists believe that willpower is sort of like a muscle; it gets stronger when you exercise it, but during the moment of exertion, it can fail if it's pushed past a certain point. Malicious people can cancel your willpower by forcing you to overexert it.

Willpower is what's makes it possible for us to make the right decisions in the face of serious temptation or pressure. It's what makes us spend time studying for an exam instead of watching videos online. Without willpower, we become highly suggestible, and people can get us to do their bidding with little resistance.

Ego depletion is sometimes also referred to as "decision fatigue." The idea behind this concept is that the more decisions we make, the more fatigued we become, and as a result, we are unable to make good decisions. When manipulative people put us in situations where we have to keep making decisions, they eventually are able to wear us out.

There are several other factors that have been known to destroy willpower. The first one is scarcity. When something is scarce, we are tempted to act in a more impulsive way to acquire it, abandoning our principles in the process. For instance, when you are hungry, you might be forced to abandon the "thou shalt not steal" principle just to feed yourself.

People who are adept at emotional manipulation can chip away at your willpower by introducing the element of scarcity. For example, when a person gives you the silent treatment, she is essentially withholding human interaction and affection, thus making it a scarcity for you. This increases the likelihood that you will abandon your stand and comply with her request.

When manipulators succeed in canceling our willpower, then they gain the power to control us and tell us what to do. We will start deferring our judgment to them, and we will lose our identities.

# Destroy self-esteem

Apart from depleting your willpower, malicious people also want to destroy your self-esteem. Unfortunately, there have dozens of different ways that they can do this. In as much as we try to draw our self-esteem from within, the fact remains that as social beings, we put a lot of stock in what other people say about us, and that is where manipulative people draw their strength.

Manipulators can chip away at your self-esteem by using carefully worded phrases that are aimed at attacking and belittling you. Their words are usually carefully calculated to either upset you or to confuse you so that you spend a lot of time thinking about what they mean. We have already looked at the kinds of manipulative techniques that can cause you to start questioning yourself or thinking that your own emotions aren't valid.

Manipulators also chip away at your self-esteem by constantly blaming you for all sorts of problems.

When someone keeps telling you that certain things are your fault, a seed of self-doubt will start growing in you, and as this idea is reinforced, you will get to a point where you start actually internalizing the person's criticism, and this ruins your self-esteem.

Sometimes, manipulative people can pass the blame onto you without even saying a word. When something bad happens, they'll give you a look that says everything you need to know about how they feel, and even in the absence of an accusation, you will start questioning yourself.

Another way manipulative people destroy your self-esteem is by flooding you with negative information. We all know that self-esteem can be affected by the company we keep. If we surround ourselves with negative people, and they keep saying bad things, we start internalizing those things. Manipulative people, especially Machiavellians, can dupe us by feeding us negative information.

Manipulative people can also destroy your self-esteem by feeding your fears. Once they discover that you have certain fears, they'll start nurturing those fears in you so that they can use them against you. The more afraid we are, the more our self-esteem diminishes.

Manipulative people like it when their victims have low self-esteem for a lot of reasons. You have probably heard the saying that if you don't stand for something, you will fall for anything. That is what manipulators are counting on here. They know that if you don't have a strong view of yourself, they can gain the power to control how you view yourself. If you start doubting who you are, they'll take over and create a version of you that they can push around.

Manipulators also know that when we have low self-esteem, we become very agreeable because we want to please other people so as to gain some positive attention and to win the approval of others. They want their victims to turn into people-pleasers, and they want to put themselves at the center of the victims' lives so that they are the ones benefiting from it.

# Passive-aggressive revenge

Some manipulators will go after you because they are seeking passive-aggressive revenge against you. If you have ever slighted a narcissistic person, a sadist, or a psychopath in any way, they are probably holding some sort of grudge against you, and they may manipulate you because they want to get even.

Now, normal people hold grudges or go after each other for clear reasons that both parties are aware of. However, people with dark personality traits can target you for pretty much any reason, as long as it makes sense to them. There is no logical threshold that you have to meet for them to set their sights on you. They could hold a grudge for years because of a statement that you made in passing. They could make you their target because your boss complimented you instead of them. They could even target you because of deep psychological issues that even they cannot comprehend.

When someone is seeking passive-aggressive revenge against you, they'll want to put you down so that they can feel superior. They think that you have it good, so they want to cut you down to size by making you feel insecure. If you outperform them at work, they'll want your performance to decline because it will make them feel better. Such people will treat you with a lot of disguised verbal hostility. They will propagate negative gossip about you when you are away. They will go out of their way to find fault in the things that you do, and they will be habitually critical of you. They'll try their best to invalidate your thoughts, feeling, and contributions because they just don't want you to be happy.

Some people will seek passive-aggressive revenge against you because they are miserable, and misery loves company. Most people with dark personality traits just can't stand seeing you happy when they are miserable.

The narcissists believe the world revolves around them, so if they are miserable, they'll expect everyone else to be miserable, and they'll try to punish anyone who isn't miserable through psychological manipulation. Sadists will try to make you miserable as a way of cheering themselves up. Machiavellians, on the other hand, will scheme to steal your happiness.

People seeking passive-aggressive revenge often use disguised hostile humor to bring others down. They use sarcasm to veil their hostility towards others. They'll say hurtful things then claim that they are "just kidding." They'll attack others based on their looks, their social-cultural background, their gender and sexual orientation, their levels of education, and anything else that comes to mind.

In other words, these manipulators have deep-seated issues which result in psychological disturbances, and they'll go out of their way to harm others in order to satisfy their psychological needs.

# Confuse reality

Manipulators also want to confuse your reality so that they can control you. Altering a person's perception of reality is the ultimate way to control and dominate them. That's because when you can convince a person that what he sees and hears isn't real, then you gain the power to tell them what they should think, what you should feel, and what you should value.

Controlling other people's reality is the ultimate dream for any manipulator. They want you to substitute your judgment for theirs, and the chances of that happening increase exponentially when you question your own reality. That is why mind control manipulation techniques, such as brainwashing and gaslighting, are the most dangerous ones.

There are lots of reasons why a manipulator would want to confuse his victim's reality. An abusive partner would want you to quit looking for help, so they would either want you to believe that you are going crazy and the abuse isn't really happening, or that no one will offer you the love and protection that you are hoping for, so you should stop searching for it.

When psychopath's gaslight others, they tend to do it intentionally. They are deliberately trying to damage their victim's mental health because they know when you are mentally weak, they can control you. They don't have a conscience, so they don't care if they do irreversible damage.

Narcissists, on the other hand, tend to gaslight others or confuse their reality unintentionally. That is because the narcissists are themselves delusional; they have delusions of grandeur, and they think that they are entitled to dominate you.

They'll confuse your reality because they want to impose their own perceptions onto you so that their delusions of grandeur can become your reality.

Bullies and sadists will want to confuse your reality because they want it to be bleak. Their intention is to make you have a pessimistic outlook, just like them.

# CHAPTER 10

# Behavior Specific Types of Emotional Manipulation

EMOTIONAL MANIPULATORS WILL ATTEMPT to take you to their "home turf," or at least to a place where they are comfortable. This tactic will eventually make it easier for them to manipulate you. A manipulative person can allow you to communicate with them at a specific location such as an office, home, or public setting.

It gives them a sense of command since before asking you there, they most likely scoped the place out. That way, while you may not know anything about the place yet, they are familiar with their surroundings. Cunning, but a simple way to gain control access for manipulators.

Manipulators will allow you to have the first say to build up your courage before addressing your weaknesses. This trick is done by numerous sales representatives when they decide if you will be the perfect candidate to buy what they are about to offer. We create a benchmark on your logic and behavior by asking general questions and evaluating them, from which they can then determine your strengths and deficiencies. This kind of concealed plan addressing can also occur in the work environment or with personal connections.

Manipulators know how to twist the truth, and they are going to get away with it because they do not always think they are lying. They are finding a way to twist the truth so much that they believe it is 100% true.

This action can occur in the forms of deception, making an argument, double-dealing, censoring the injured person for causing their abuse, distortion of reality, disclosure or retention of vital information, misrepresentation, a modest portrayal of the facts, and seeing only the truth in their narrative.

Sometimes manipulators will overwhelm you by presenting you with a great deal of knowledge, sometimes in a confusing way. They exploit you by feeding yourself with false claims, measurements, and other information that you may not care about or investigate yourself.

In deals and financial circumstances, in conversations at the expert level, or social interactions, this can happen.

The manipulator creates the perfect opportunity to snare you by assuming control over you. Some people use this system to have a sense of academic predominance.

Manipulators also find ways to overwhelm you formally. Which means they are going to blame their decisions on rules or regulations, and events that seem to be outside their control. Many people use administration— desk work, procedures, rules, consulting teams, and various forms of government to advance their strategy of trying to make you fall for their deception scheme.

This method can also be used to postpone reality discovery, conceal imperfections and weaknesses, and sidestep examination. Your employer could make you work on a holiday and justify that he could not do something, even though he could have made the same change himself. This approach is like saying, "I would if I could," although the manipulator can change the situation.

A manipulator often raises his voice and displays negative emotions. This action can be a powerful control device. If they complain loudly enough or express negative feelings that are out of proportion to a situation, most reasonable people would succumb to their threats and give them what they need, if not for a better reason, to maintain peace. The strong voice is usually accompanied by solid non-verbal communication, such as standing movements or energized motions to enhance conflict.

Surprise may choose to use another can technique manipulator. We may use an outrageous statement when telling a story, such as "you will never believe what the other person has done to me." They also use incredible assertions such as, "I was the only one doing any work today." These paint a surprising situation that can catch off guard the other person, more likely to fall for the increased truths that the manipulator shares.

The sudden negative information regularly comes unexpectedly, so you only have to plan and counter for a short time. You may be asked by the controller for additional concessions to keep working with you.

In some situations, a manipulator might not even allow you to choose. This action is a standard contract and agreement technique where you depend on the controller to decide on an option before you get ready.

A manipulator will have high expectations of you and demand high demands, bearing in mind that you may not be able to do what they request. They'll make it look like it is not even an option to say "no," although it might be unfair in the first place what they are asking of you.

Manipulators expect you to break and surrender to the demands of the manipulator by applying pressure and power. Rather than asking, "Do you think you can do that?" They are always going to ask, "When can you do that?" The manipulator never gives you the chance to decide to do something first. It makes it difficult for you to say "no" to anything for which they might be asking.

Manipulators will indulge cynical cleverness aimed at exploiting your vulnerabilities and will attempt to undermine you. They are going to make sarcastic jokes to knock you down, and when you are offended by these terms, they are going to say, "I was just joking," or "No big deal." Manipulators like to make simple statements, sometimes disguised in witness or collegiality, to depict victims as second-rate or weak. These remarks relate to appearance, personality, experience, credentials, and even how you strolled into work late by two minutes.

The attacker wants to establish control over you by making you look bad and making you feel terrible. In an attempt to point out things about you that could affect how others view you, they also do this. While you may enjoy some musician that others do not think about, a manipulator might say something like, "How could anyone like that band?" The silent treatment is a popular manipulator tool; they know it may be the best way to get under your skin by being ignored. By deliberately not responding to your calls, messages, or requests, the manipulator assumes control by making you pause and place uncertainty and vulnerability in your mind. Sometimes silence can be the most powerful weapon.

The manipulator may not personally give you the silent treatment, but they may claim to forget you, so you do not know their intentions. The manipulator makes you take on what is her duty and makes you sweat with effort and anxiety by pretending that she does not understand what you need or what you need her to do.

Kids use this technique to postpone assignments, delay demands on them, and force grown-ups to do what the child would like not to do for them. This strategy is also used by some adults when they have a task they want to ignore or a commitment they want to avoid. For instance, doing a deliberately bad job mopping the floor can trick the person in charge to decide not to delegate the task to you again.

This action can mean, on a larger scale, someone in a relationship pretends to be unaware of what you might need on an emotional level. Manipulators are going to say things like, "I do not understand what you are going to want," even though they know very well what you need and just do not want to get into the work to achieve that aim.

This action leads to how often you are going to be guilt-tripped by manipulators. Other examples might include blaming others instead of themselves, dwelling on their failures, behaving as if someone else holds the key to their success and accomplishment, or despair and deceit. The controller pressures the recipient into surrender by focusing on guilt-tripping others.

Then manipulators will make sure the victim plays no matter how wrong it may be. Some examples of this type of behavior include over-represented or imagined individual issues, misrepresented or manufactured medical problems, reliance, codependency, conscious fragility to inspire compassion and support, and frail or weak playing.

The motive for victim-playing manipulators is often to exploit the sympathy of the victim, feelings of guilt, feelings of duty and loyalty, or eagerness to protect and help, to extricate ludicrous advantages and concessions.

The term "gaslighting" is often used to refer to manipulation that causes individuals to address themselves, their existence, memories, or musings. Gaslighting occurs when someone tries to make you feel crazy so that they can get away with manipulative behavior.

A manipulative person can change what you are saying and make it all about them, catch the conversation, or make you feel compelled to do something bad when you have done nothing wrong.

You may feel a misguided sense of guilt when you are gaslighted that you have done something terrible, even if that is not the case. Manipulators blame; in any case, they never admit responsibility.

Instead, if you let a manipulator know they hurt your feelings, they'll point out how crazy you are, remember things wrong, or be too sensitive to the situation.

You can almost be sure that you are being used as soon as someone does you a favor, not for the sake of "just because" but with hidden motives. An effective manipulator can be called "Mr. Nice Guy". This person can be helpful to other people and complete a lot of favors. Yet there is a string attached to every great deed— a desire. If you do not satisfy the desire or intent of the manipulator, you will be identified as irrational.

For example, a sales rep, even though they do not think the item suits you, might influence your decision to buy a clothing item. The manipulator can send you flowers right before asking you for a favor in a relationship. Since they misuse social standards, these strategies work. It is normal to respond to favors, but we still feel constrained to accept and go along when someone delivers one misleadingly.

## EXERCISE:

ARE YOU A MANIPULATOR?

Can you get people to do what you want? Find out with this test if you're a manipulator?

1.  There's nothing wrong with telling a little lie to avoid trouble.

2.  It's a great move to flatter the important people who are in a position to help me.

3.  When I was a kid, I was bossy.

4.  In this very competitive society, every means is permissible to move forward.

5.  Most people are honest and loyal.

6.  P.T. Barnum was right when he said: every minute an imbecile comes into the world.

7.  You can't go on with all the rules.

8.  Most people are brave.

9.  The main difference between those caught breaking the law and others is that the former were not smart enough not to be discovered.

10. You should never tell anyone the real reason why things are done unless it serves to achieve the goal.

CALCULATE THE SCORE:

To calculate your score, assign 1 point to each answer equal to yours.

1. True  2. True  3. True  4. True  5. False  6. True  7. True
8. False  9. True  10. True

3 points down: you're not a manipulator at all and you take the opinions of others in high regard. You always try to smooth things out and sometimes you even give the impression that you surrender too easily.

4 to 6 points: you're average. Defend your ideas to the full, but not to the point of overpowering or manipulating others.

7 points up: six Machiavellian. You have very personal opinions about rights and duties and you hate any form of approval. You don't think you need to blunt a few angular corners of your character here and there.

# CHAPTER 11
# Signs That You're Being Manipulated

IN THE EVENT THAT UNADDRESSED, control can prompt poor emotional wellness results for the individuals who are controlled. Incessant control in cozy connections may likewise be a sign psychological mistreatment is occurring, which at times, can have a comparable impact to injury—especially when the casualty of control is made to feel regretful or embarrassed.

Casualties of incessant control may:

- Feel discouraged
- Develop nervousness
- Develop undesirable adapting designs
- Constantly attempt to satisfy the manipulative individual

- Lie about their emotions
- Put someone else's needs before their own
- Find it hard to confide in others

Now and again, control can be inescapable to such an extent that it makes an injured individual inquiry their view of the real world. The exemplary motion picture Gaslight outlined one such story, in which a lady's significant other quietly controlled her until she never again confided in her very own discernment. For instance, the spouse clandestinely turned down the gaslights and persuaded his better half the diminishing light was all in her mind.

# Specific Examples of Emotional Manipulation

# 1. The Secret Techniques of the Best Salespeople

- **Taking the advisor role**

The best salespeople never come across as though they are trying to sell you something right out the gate. They approach as though they are your advisor, guiding you to finding the best product for you.

This is the best way to avoid putting your customer or client on edge and increasing the chances they will buy something. Look carefully at the approach of the person who tries to sell you something and note how they use this technique to try to put you at ease and make you more suggestible.

- **Listening skills**

The best salespeople know how to listen closely for the smallest detail that might help them close the deal. It might be a sign of hesitation, confidence anything that tells them if you are a target, they should be spending their time on and how they should know if it is time to move on.

Usually, we end up being the ones to give these salespeople all the information they need to handle us better. All they usually have to do is listen as we over-answer simple questions and give ourselves away.

- **Empathy**

A salesperson who can get under the skin of a prospective client is often more likely to have higher sales because they are able to build a far better rapport with the people they interact with and make them feel safe and secure.

Consider this technique the when you encounter a salesperson you considered particularly likable. They may just have been using a sense of empathy to comfort you into buying something you may not have wanted in the first place.

- **Assuming the sale**

Salespeople these days no longer ask you if you want to buy their product or not. More often than not they will ask for your details and ask you to sign on the dotted line as if you already agreed to make the purchase.

This often tricks a lot of people into buying things since they don't realize they are being baited into buying something until they're already signing. This tactic is also useful because it takes the choice away from the buyer and puts it in the salesperson's hands.

- ## **Confidence**

People are a lot more likely to buy with their feelings than with their heads, so a confident salesperson can be highly effective because people are more likely to want to trust them simply because of their confident demeanor.

It's natural to want to follow the lead of someone when they seem like they know exactly where they are going. Salespeople use this information to the fullest by starting the sale with a confident body language that engages you even before any words have been spoken.

- ## **Honesty (where possible)**

One of many tactics' salespeople have in common with attorneys is their ability to manipulate the truth. They know how to omit certain truths or simply bend the truth where possible to ensure you see the picture the way they want you to.

They will tell the truth where possible and avoid it where necessary. As long as it benefits them, they will play with the truth as much as possible while maintaining a sense of plausible deniability. This way they can practice deception without lying. They escape on a technicality.

- ## **Curiosity**

Great salespeople will often use questions that seem simple to get what they want from you. They may disguise these questions as simple curiosity, but they are usually laying the groundwork properly to manipulate you into buying what they want.

In the game of persuasion, information is king. The more you know about a target, the more ammunition you have to bypass their rational mind and appeal to their emotions. No word must be wasted, and all information must be treasured.

## • Adaptability

The best salespeople you ever come across will often behave like chameleons. They will observe you and switch whatever details about themselves they need to in order to get under your skin and pull you in. They mold their sales pitch around you.

Getting you to feel comfortable enough to listen and give them more and more of your time is a classic sales technique that ensures that nothing as small as beliefs, moods and/or ideologies impede getting what they want, your money.

## • Communication skills

It is imperative that a salesperson has the gift of the gab and is quick on their feet because the customers will spend more time listening to the way a salesperson speaks more than they do the actual content of their speech.

Therefore, you will often find that the best salespeople will make subtle changes to the way they use language to better appeal to whoever is in front of them at that moment.

## • Escalating

Escalation is a great tactic that slowly gets you from the sales floor to the office where the papers await your signature. It involves slowly filling your hands with things or carefully orchestrating the tour so that you finally end up at the office, isolated and comfortable.

This also works well after the sale when one might call you and follow up or maybe even try to get new leads through you. Slowly escalating sets the customer at ease enough to not notice that things are not moving at the pace they intended.

- **Preparation for objections**

As with anything in life, preparation is key. Preparing for possible objections is common among the best attorneys and salespeople. This is a great way to establish and reinforce your position as the expert who needs to be trusted in this given field.

Salespeople take care to make sure they give you the sense that they know more than you and once that has entered your mind, it becomes of the utmost import that they maintain that guise by having all the answers to your questions.

- **Patience**

Patience is a commonly used sales tactic that is seldom recognized by prospective clients. Selling is a process, not an action. The best salespeople will delay you to the point where it becomes a war of attrition.

You could easily be stuck in a salesperson's office for several minutes at a time as they go around finalizing this and verifying that. Do not fall for this trick. It is only to wear down your patience and have you willing to do almost anything to feel the relief of seeing things moving forward, wherever that might lead.

- **Passion**

A passionate and enthusiastic salesmen or woman is usually worth a lot to the company they work for because such energetic and positive people can easily sink their hooks into the emotions of their clients and have them follow them down an emotional rabbit-hole that leads them far from the realms of logic where they may easily lose a sale.

Watch out for this kind of approach. Someone coming across as enthusiastic and passionate about what they are speaking about may have that and nothing else. Keep such people focused on the facts and you could find yourself taking the dominant position in these kinds of discussions.

- **Charm**

Charm, much like passion, is a common attribute a lot of the best salespeople in the game learn to master and weaponize. People are more likely to trust people they feel they get along with than they will someone they could not picture themselves enjoying an unrelated social interaction with.

This is one of the oldest tricks known as it makes you feel it is permissible to let down your guard and trust the individual in front of you. You do so at your own peril.

It is good to remember that there is power in knowing when to appear vulnerable and when to appear strong, but it is always good for those who follow you to think you are always honest with them.

This can be achieved by picking moments where people feel like they can reach you and communicate with you if necessary, but you have to control this, so it never works against or inconveniences you. Selectively opening your door to those you lead and knowing when to show weakness to them- but only when it can't be used against you- is a powerful tool in making people feel listened to and that they can trust you.

# 2. Factors That Make You Vulnerable to Manipulation

People often make themselves very vulnerable to other people. However, most of the time, they'll only do this as a reaction. If you'll be the first to make yourself 'vulnerable,' then you can often get them to open up as well. This can be a great way to learn how to get under their skin, as well as to learn what sort of tactics you need to use to influence them.

There are two different routes that you can take here. The first is people know about you. This has a few consequences but also a few perks. The most obvious consequence is that this opens you up to being emotionally vulnerable to the other person. If you can't shut your emotions off completely, then you may find yourself growing attached to them. This isn't good if you just want to use them for gaining something.

On the other hand, depending on the stories that you shared, this might mean that people may corroborate with you if you ever need them. I would personally have a few stories on reserve that don't particularly matter if they get out, because if someone realizes that you're using them, they may get angry and retaliate by leaking your 'secrets' if they're immature.

The second route is that you can make up stories. This one is best done over the phone or in person rather than through e-mail or text message. If you make up stories, then you can rest easy that they have no actual attachment to you in a real sense. You may even set up a reserve of fake stories for different situations.

An added benefit of this method is that if they decide to leak your secrets, so long as you don't leave a paper trail, you can accuse them of making up things to defame you since nobody will be able to corroborate what they're saying about you. This also serves as the primary drawback, though. If you need somebody to corroborate your own story, you either have to go without it or let somebody know that you're trying to use somebody else, which can cause a bunch of problems in and of itself.

All in all, though, if you can make yourself vulnerable to another person, they will begin to feel an attachment to you, and they will take everything that you tell them more seriously.

## WRAP IT UP

All effective actions have the same structure—a sequence of stages—the absence of any of which dramatically (sometimes to zero) reduces the likelihood of success. The impact, built clearly on this structure, is triggered with the greatest possible probability—true, not one hundred percent. The impact, I repeat, refers to any and in any field—in politics, in business, in personal relationships, in sports, in war, in religion. If the effect worked, you are very likely to find a familiar structure in it.

Individual sentences may go beyond the grammar of the basic English language, yet, everything is correct. The laws of neuro-linguistic programming, dark psychology and manipulation dictate their own ways of dealing with words. And it is quite possible that all these nuances will be noticed only by the editor, but not by you.

Some topics and thoughts will be repeated more than once. Sometimes in the same words.

At the first reading, I recommend just to believe: it is necessary. The second reading will give you several times more information: you will already understand what and why I am doing in this book. A third reading will show that the bottom here is not double, but triple.

And at some point, you will find that you too can. And perhaps you will be surprised that you once thought that it was difficult.

# CHAPTER 12

# Difference Between Manipulation and Persuasion

WHILE PEOPLE WHO CONTROL OTHERS frequently do so in light of the fact that they want to control their condition and environment and urge that regularly originates from profound situated fear or uneasiness, it's anything but solid conduct. Taking part in manipulation may keep the manipulator from associating with their bona fide self and being controlled can make an individual encounter a wide scope of sick impacts.

Manipulation infers twisting reality so as to get somebody to plan something inverse for their underlying goal. This is an activity proposed to get the other individual to plan something useful for just one of the gatherings in question – for the most part, the one controlling.

Promoters control individuals into deduction; they need an item and that they have to remain hip and well known at any age.

Everything goes with regards to manipulation and having any type of influence is a decent device. Youngsters regularly control their folks. Indeed, even since the beginning, they can interface their folks' regard for their mentality, and they can counterfeit trouble so as to get consideration or compensations of any kind. In any case, enthusiastic manipulation is utilized on all levels throughout everyday life, not just in youth.

Manipulation likewise feels constrained. There is a sure degree of pressure included with regards to it. At the point when the underlying legitimate contentions fizzle, the conversation may get individual.

The individual being controlled is cornered into a spot where they feel like there is no other path; however, to take the choice exhibited by the controller.

# Psychological Wellness Effects of Manipulation

On the off chance that unaddressed, manipulation can prompt poor psychological wellness results for the individuals who are controlled. Incessant manipulation in cozy connections may likewise be a sign psychological mistreatment is occurring, which at times, can have a comparable impact to injury—especially when the casualty of manipulation is caused to feel blameworthy or embarrassed.

Casualties of interminable manipulation may:

- Feel discouraged

- Develop tension

- Develop undesirable adapting designs

- Constantly attempt to satisfy the manipulative individual

- Lie about their emotions

- Put someone else's needs before their own

- Find it hard to confide in others

Now and again, manipulation can be unavoidable to the point that it makes an unfortunate casualty question their view of the real world. The exemplary motion picture Gaslight represented one such story, in which a lady's better half unpretentiously controlled her until she never again confided in her own recognitions. For instance, the spouse secretly turned down the gaslights and convinced his better half the diminishing light was all in her mind.

# Manipulation in Relationships

Long haul manipulation can have genuine impacts on cozy connections, including those between companions, relatives, and sentimental accomplices. Manipulation can break down the wellbeing of a relationship and lead to poor psychological wellness of those in the relationship or even the disintegration of the relationship.

In a marriage or association, manipulation can make one accomplice feel tormented, segregated, or useless. Indeed, even in solid connections, one accomplice may unintention-ally control the other so as to maintain a strategic distance from an encounter or even trying to shield their accomplice from feeling troubled. Numerous people may even realize they are being controlled in their relationship and decide to neglect or minimize it. Manipulation in personal connec-tions can take numerous structures, including distortion, blame, blessing giving, or specifically demonstrating love, mystery keeping, and latent animosity.

Guardians who control their kids may set their youngsters up for blame, melancholy, tension, eating issues, and other psychological well-being conditions. One investigation addi-tionally uncovered that guardians who consistently use ma-nipulation tactics on their kids might improve the probability their kids will likewise utilize manipulative conduct. Indica-tions of manipulation in the parent-kid relationship may in-corporate, causing the kid to feel blameworthy, absence of responsibility from a parent, making light of a youngster's accomplishments, and a should be engaged with numerous parts of the kid's life.

People may likewise feel controlled in the event that they are a piece of a fellowship that has gotten dangerous. In ma-nipulative kinships, one individual might be utilizing the other to address their own issues to the detriment of their friends.

A manipulative companion may utilize blame or compul-sion to separate favors, for example, crediting cash, or they may possibly contact that companion when they need their own passionate needs met and may discover pardons when their companion has needs in the relationship.

# Instances of Manipulative Behavior

Some of the time, people may control others unwittingly, without being completely mindful of what they're doing, while others may effectively take a shot at reinforcing their manipulation tactics. A few indications of manipulation include:

- Passive-forceful conduct
- Implicit dangers
- Dishonesty
- Withholding data
- Isolating an individual from friends and family
- Gaslighting
- Verbal misuse
- Use of sex to accomplish objectives

As the thought processes behind manipulation can shift from oblivious to malignant, it's critical to recognize the conditions of the manipulation that is occurring. While severing things might be basic in circumstances of misuse, a specialist may help other people figure out how to manage or go up against manipulative conduct from others.

# The most effective method to Deal with Manipulative People

At the point when manipulation gets poisonous, managing the conduct from others can be debilitating. Manipulation in the working environment has been appeared to lessen execution, and manipulative conduct from friends and family can cause reality to appear to be faulty. I you believe you are being controlled in any sort of a relationship; it might be useful to:

- Disengage. If somebody is attempting to get a specific enthusiastic reaction from you, decide not to offer it to them. For instance, if a manipulative companion is known to compliment you before requesting an exceeding kindness, don't cooperate—rather, answer cordially and move the discussion along.

- Be sure. Here and there, manipulation may incorporate one individual's endeavors to make someone else question their capacities, instinct, or even reality. In the event that this occurs, it might assist with keeping up with your account; in any case, if this happens regularly in a cozy relationship, it could be an ideal opportunity to leave.

- Address the circumstance. Get out the manipulative conduct as it's going on. Maintaining the attention on how the other individual's activities are influencing you instead of beginning with an accusatory explanation may likewise assist you with arriving at goals while underlining that their manipulative tactics won't chip away at you.

- Stay on-subject. At the point when you call attention to conduct that causes you to feel controlled, the other individual may attempt to limit the circumstance or jumble the circumstance by raising different issues as an interruption. Recollect your primary concern and adhere to that.

# Tending to Manipulation in Therapy

Treatment and therapy for manipulative conduct may generally rely upon what hidden issues are causing the conduct. for example, the manipulation is being brought about by a fundamental psychological wellness issue, singular therapy may enable that individual to comprehend why their conduct is undesirable for themselves and everyone around them. A guide may likewise have the option to enable the manipulative individual to learn abilities for collaborating with others while regarding their limits and address fundamental frailties that might be adding to the conduct.

Certain psychological wellness issues, for example, the marginal character, may make people feel uneasiness seeing someone, making them act manipulatively so as to have a sense of safety. On these occasions, a specialist may enable the individual to address their psychological well-being issue, which thusly can lessen their uneasiness and assist them with having a sense of safety in their connections.

# The Art of Persuasion

Persuasion as an art should be subtle and unnoticed. Less forceful than manipulation, more palatable than coercion, persuasion carries with it the assumption that, those persuaded act out of their own 'fully informed' will and usually in a way that works towards the embitterment of all involved. This is not necessarily the case, however, framing an idea in an altruistic way of thinking is a good place to start. The following methods of persuasion are focused on being passive in our persuasion, we wait for the right time, consider their feelings, their values and standpoints.

These tactics compliment and support each other to create a strategy that is practically impossible to see through and so cannot be directly argued against or attacked with violating socially agreed upon rules of conduct.

- Using an honorable cause is a great way to get someone's attention but an honorable cause alone is rarely enough to convert others to your way of thinking, to truly convert them we must shift their focus away from the cause to their own self-interest. Linking a great cause to the self-interest of listeners is an overwhelmingly powerful motivator. Once the listener begins to think about what they may get out of modifying their opinions or reassessing their loyalties the cage door is closed.

- As a rule, anyone can be persuaded of anything providing the timing, approach and context are correct but there are limitations such as time constraints. Prior to any attempt at persuasion, analyze the context of the situation as a whole and devise an approach that is acceptable and based around the current underlying mood or general atmosphere, otherwise known as the emotional 'flow' of the situation. Do not go against the flow of the situation, instead use the emotional flow to your advantage. Frame your ideas as exciting when people are jovial and as safe and pre-emptive in times of reflection. Going with the flow in this way allows you to syphon the already existing emotions in the room directly into your initiative. This method is ultimately more effective than simple trying to change the topic of conversation to one that serves your purpose.

- Timing is another pivotal factor when persuading others. The time of day greatly affects the expected desires of any particular person, for example, if we try to corner someone at work at 4pm on a Friday afternoon it is likely that all they can think about is leaving work for the weekend and so a large part of their brain will have already left the building. This could work to our advantage or against it depending on the goal. The timing of an approach extends beyond hours and days to weeks, months, and years, the longer ahead we can plan the greater our overall chances of success.

- Identify those individuals who are 'on the fence' or easy to influence and concentrate your efforts on these individuals in the same way that politicians focus on 'swing' voters.

- Most people are their own worst enemy, give them enough rope and they will only be too happy to tie the noose. Ask questions that get people talking and they will quickly voice opinions and values that can then be mirrored back at them in the present or used eventually to obtain their consent. Being cordial will cause people to open up to you and in doing so they will provide the information needed to devise an approach that speaks directly to their personally held beliefs and values, at which point they will be powerless to refuse you or refute your way of thinking.

# CHAPTER 13

# What is Persuasion?

THERE ARE MANY TIMES WHEN THE HUMAN mind is pretty easy to influence, but it does take a certain set of skills to get people to stop and listen to you. Not everyone is good with influence and persuasion, though. They can talk all day and would not be able to convince others to do what they want. On the other hand, there are those who could persuade anyone to do what they want, even if they had just met this person for the first time. Knowing how to work with these skills will make it easier for you to recognize a manipulator and be better prepared to avoid them if needed.

The first thing that we need to look at is what persuasion is. Persuasion is simply the process or action taken by a person or a group of people when they want to cause something to change. This could be in relation to another human being and something that changes in their inner mental systems or their external behavior patterns.

# The Three Emissaries of Public Opinion Modern Day Aristotle

## 1. Ethos

This technique portrays the speaker as an ethically qualified expert on the topic in question. In most cases, the speaker has titles that reinforce this idea, such as a professor or master. This title builds the audience's trust in the speaker. The presenter may use the following strategies to convince and persuade the audience.

- Showing unmatched mastery of the topic. This is demonstrated through the use of various terminologies associated with the topic. Some of these terminologies are strange to the audience

- Being introduced by established authorities to speak to the audience. This attaches more importance to the person, thus increasing the amount of respect they command from the audience.

- Their command of language is flawless. The speech characterized by heavy vocabulary. Their use of grammar and articulation of words leaves the audience in awe. This makes it hard not to listen and heed their words.

They show a fair-minded approach and analysis of ideas. The presenter shows sincerity to the audience by giving proof and

- Illustrations to give credulity to their ideas. They also attach a lot of logic and reasoning to their speech.

- Sharing a list of their accomplishments with the audience as a way of gaining more credibility. This is mostly accompanied by evidence such as referring the audience to the internet to search for those achievements.

Combining all these tactics yields tremendous results when it comes to persuading their audience. The effectiveness of this method arises from the ignorance of the audience. The speaker uses this ignorance to manipulate their minds into thinking they are being educated. Even those that got some insight into the topic are neutralized by the supposedly superior knowledge of the presenter. This technique is used in dark psychology to introduce manipulative concepts into the minds of the audience after weakening their reasoning ability.

The example below illustrates the use of the concept of ethos as a persuasion technique in dark psychology.

*"As you have been told by your chief, I am the manager in charge of marketing and recruitment. I understand most of you don't have jobs. I will give you a little story about myself. I started selling herbal medicine when I was still a first year in university. I couldn't secure a job for over a year after leaving school despite my high grades. Lee introduced me to Precious Nature Company Int. five years ago, a world-famous enterprise that has given hope to tens of thousands of hopeless souls. I was asked to make an investment of thirty thousand dollars alongside a registration fee of twenty dollars. I didn't earn anything for the first three months, but my earnings started growing from the fourth month. Right now, I earn half a million dollars every month without commissions of the people I have brought to join the company. That Mercedes you see outside is worth fif-*

*ty thousand dollars, and it was bought with commissions only. I am here to show you how."*

We can see all the features of ethos in this short speech. The speaker is persuading his audience to join some pyramid scheme. Not all businesses that operate like this are pyramid schemes, but most pyramid schemes operate this way. The speaker has been introduced by the chief, a figure of authority. The speaker's title is also indicated, a big title for that matter. The speaker shows that he is willing to help them make a fortune just like he did; he even shows them the evidence- a ten-million-dollar Mercedes Benz. Due to the level of respect the speaker commands under his title, accomplishments, and 'knowledge' of the subject, coupled with the audience's desperate situation of joblessness, the probability of the audience doing as the speaker asks is very high.

# 2. Logos

This is the use of facts and figures to support the speaker's thesis. The term 'logos' is derived from the word 'logic' which involves the use of reason to give weight to ideas. The presenter may exaggerate these facts and figures as a way of convincing and confusing the audience. Logos also reinforces ethos since the presenter looks more knowledgeable to the audience by simply applying logic in their presentation. In the world of dark psychology, the kind of reasoning used is marred with inaccuracies, falsified or non-contextualized data, outright misrepresentation of facts, and generally misleading information.

Logos is a technique of persuasion in dark psychology that has the following features.

- The speaker is more theoretical in their speech. This makes it difficult to ascertain some of their claims, but the target audience believes them anyway. The strategy is meant to keep the audience in the dark until the agent gets whatever they want from them. The agent is afraid of giving practical examples because the probability of tripping over is quite high, a situation that is made worse by the lack of credibility of those ideas.

- Widespread use of abstract language. Their speech is characterized by numerously concealed facts meant to deliberately keep the target audience off-balance. This concealment is achieved through the use of difficult vocabulary that's hard for the audience to understand. The language is simply too technical for the common man. Very few people dare to ask questions on something they have very little understand of in the first place.

- The agent uses wrong or inaccurate definitions most of the time. This works by further misleading the audience about the subject at hand. The speaker will deliberately twist the meaning of some terminologies to align them with their objective. The audience might not object to this deliberate non-contextualization because of the low level of the grasp they have on the subject. This leaves them vulnerable to persuasion and manipulation.

Extensive use of citations and quotations. The speaker will refer to the works of experts and authorities as a way of reinforcing their persuasion. Dark psychologists would often make their quotations and citations based on imaginary or inaccurate sources.

The following example illustrates the concept of logos concerning dark psychology.

"We have made tremendous steps as a government in ensuring equitable distribution of natural resources. The wells and oil refinery in this region alone have provided jobs to over ten thousand people in the last two years, the majority of them being youths. At this rate, it means there will be over a hundred thousand jobs created in ten years. We also want to ensure every household has electricity by the end of the following year. Data collected by a renowned American research firm indicates that countries that have reached this milestone in power provision have a life expectancy above 80 years. Think of it like this, the retirement age in this country is sixty years. With a life expectancy of eighty years, it means you have around twenty years left in your pocket to enjoy the retirement benefits and watch your children grow. But what happens when you die early? There is something called psychological trauma, which is the inability of the brain to grow and think properly due to a sad event. This is what your loved ones will undergo when you leave them that early. As you may be aware, 10 percent of all deaths worldwide are a result of psychological trauma. Let us help the government meet these goals by paying our taxes generously. What is an addition of 5 percent compared to the many benefits that come with it?"

This government official is trying to persuade people to pay an additional 5 percent in taxes to support government projects. There are many flows in this speech that only point at some mischief. The area is endowed with a natural resource that is even refined there, but it is still marginalized, residents don't have access to electricity. The speaker is presenting unverifiable information and crooked reasoning where the promise of a better future is based on his assumptions and is also tied to acceptance of extra tax the government wants. The residents might end up being persuaded based on the speaker's use of 'logic' to lure them and not because it is the right thing to do.

# 3. Pathos

This is a method of persuasion where the presenter uses the audience's emotional appeal to advance their agenda. This technique invokes strong feelings and emotions among the audience. It is designed to make the target act in a certain way as a result of emotional provocation. Dark psychologists have used this technique to drive people into acting impulsively without due consideration of the outcome of their actions. Some of the feelings a presenter invokes in the audience include anger, extreme happiness, pity, and fear. The presence of these feelings reduces the effectiveness of thinking and reasoning by a huge margin. The following features are associated with the device of pathos in the world of dark psychology.

- Use of a vivid and concrete language. This is designed to create a visualization of the subject in the audience's minds. The language involves a lot of illustrations and descriptions using objects the audience is most familiar with.

- Emotionally loaded tone and language. The kind of language the speaker uses draws pity from the audience; these feelings then generate anger and a fierce reaction. With such charged emotions, the target audience can do almost anything they are asked after that meeting.

- There is too much figurative language. The audience is left to relate what the speaker is talking about and un-cover the real event. This way, the target audience will have an exaggerated picture of the event or situation. This motivates them to react exactly the way the pre-senter expected.

- The lengthy narration of emotional events. This is meant to reinforce the emotional attachment of the matter by the audience. The longer the narration lasts, the more the emotions run high among the audience, and the faster they will give a response.

## EXERCISE:

Identify and increase your range of persuasion skills

www.mindtools.com/pages/article/influencing-skills-quiz.htm

# CHAPTER 14

# The Psychology of Persuasion

There are six main principles in the psychology of persuasion. The first principle of influence that you can use is known as reciprocity.

## Reciprocity

This is based on the idea that when you offer something to someone, they will feel a bit indebted to you and will want to reciprocate it back. Humans are wired to be this way to survive. For the manipulator to use this option, they will make sure that they are doing some kind of favor for their target. Whether that is paying them some compliments, giving them a ride to work, helping out with a big project or getting them out of trouble. Once the favor is done, the target will feel like they owe a debt to the manipulator. The manipulator will then be able to ask for something, and it will be really hard for the target to say no.

# Commitment/consistency

It is in the nature of humans to settle for what is already tried and tested in the mind. Most of us have a mental image of who we are and how things should be. And most people are not going to be willing to experiment, so they will keep on acting the way that they did in the past. So, to get them to work with this principle and do what you want, you first need to get them to commit to something. The steps that you would need to follow to get your target to do what you want through commitment and consistency include:

- Start out with something small. You can ask the target to do something small, something that is easier to manage the change, before they start to integrate it more into their personality and get hooked on the habit.

- You can get the target to accept something publicly so that they will feel more obligated to see it through.

- Reward the target when they can stick to the course. Rewards will be able to help strengthen the interest of the target in the course of action that you want them to do.

# Social proof

This is another one that will rely on the human tendency, and it relies on the fact that people place a lot of value and trust in other people and in their opinions on things that we have not tried yet. This can be truer if the information comes from a close friend or a person who is perceived as the expert.

It is impossible to try out everything in life and having to rely on others can put us at a disadvantage. This means that we need to find a reliable source to help us get started. A manipulator may be able to get someone to do something by acting as a close friend or an expert. They are able to get the target to try out a course of action because they have positioned themselves as the one who knows the most about the situation or the action.

# Authority

If you want to make sure that you can influence another person, then you need to dress and act the part. This means that you should wear clothes, as well as accessories, that will help you look like you are the one in command.
Some of the ways that you can do this include:

- Wear clothes that are befitting to what people will perceive an authoritative figure would wear.

- When you communicate with the target, you need to do so in a commanding fashion.

- Make sure that you can use the lexicon and the language of experts in that field.

When you can position yourself as the authority figure, people will look to you for the answers that they need. It does not matter how well they know you or not. You will have a great opportunity to influence them the way that you want them to behave.

# Liking

We all know that it is easy to feel attracted to a certain set of people. This can extend to friends and family members as well. So, if you would like to get others to like you and be open to persuasion from you, you first need to figure out how to go from an acquaintance to a friend. This will work similarly to the reciprocity that we talked about earlier, but some of the basic steps that you will need to follow to make this work include:

- The attraction phase: You need to make sure that there is something about you that instantly draws the other person to you.

- Make yourself relatable: People are more likely to be drawn to you if you are relatable to them in some way. It is also easier to influence another person if they consider you their friend.

- Communicate like a friend: Even if the two of you are not quite friends yet, you will be able to make use of the right communication skills so that the target will associate you as a friend.

Make it look like you are both in the same groups and that you are fighting for the same causes; this can make it easier to establish a rapport with them.

# Scarcity

The last weapon that you can use for persuasion is known as scarcity. Humans like the idea of being exclusive and are drawn to anything that they are not necessarily able to find anywhere else.

When you make something exclusive, you have a chance of making it appear more valuable. People are also going to become fearful when something they desire starts to disappear. This whole idea is part of the supply and demand principle. If you have something that is abundant, then it will be perceived as having a lower value and cheap. But if it is rare, then it must have a higher value and be more expensive.

This can work for human beings and for products in the same way. Some things that you should keep in mind when you want to use the scarcity principle with persuasion include:

- Always imply that the thing you are offering is not going to be available to the target anywhere else.

- If you can, it is a good idea to implement a countdown timer on what you are offering. This gives a physical indicator to the target that what you are offering is truly going to disappear.

- You should never go back on the stipulations that you said in the beginning. You need to make sure that the target knows that what you offered is scarce, or this method is not going to work very well.

All of these principles can be effective ways for you to be able to use persuasion to manipulate your target. It is important to learn how to use them all and to do so in a covert way so that your target is not able to realize what you are doing.

When you are successful with bringing all of this together, you are sure to get the results that you want each time.

# Tips and Practice of Persuasion Techniques

Experts say that people who are good leaders and who have good persuasion powers will utilize the following techniques to help them be successful:

- Exchanging

- Stating

- Legitimizing

- Logical persuasion

- Appealing to value

- Modeling

- Alliance building

- Consulting

- Socializing

- Appealing to a relationship

The above options are all positive ways that you can use persuasion to your advantage. Most people will be amenable to these happening. But on the other side, there are four negative tactics of persuasion that you can do as well. These would include options like manipulating, avoiding, intimidating, and threatening. These negative tactics will be easier for the target to recognize, which is why most manipulators will avoid using them if possible.

Now, you can use some of the tactics above, but according to psychologist Robert Cialdini, there are six major principles of persuasion that can help you to get the results that you want without the target being able to notice what is going on. Let us take a look at these six weapons and how they can be effective.

The best persuaders are innately curious about the world around them and the people with whom they interact. Learn what others need on a physical as well as emotional level and why. Always ask good questions and then listen.

Begin open-ended discussions that start with "Tell me...." Demonstrate a genuine interest in others and get to know their desires, dreams and goals.

Once you understand a person's position, you'll be better equipped to persuade him.

1. Use your strengths

2. Find common ground

3. Solve a problem

4. Prepare for arguments

5. Be persistent

6. Do your research

7. Take notes

8. Use names often

9. Use "mirroring"

10. Be confident

11. Be curious

12. Listen effectively

13. Be honest

14. Tell a story

15. Address concerns

16. Make your voice more effective

17. Show empathy

CHAPTER 15

# Dark Persuasion Methods: NLP

**W**HAT IS NLP? Neuro-Linguistic Programming has to do with the study of thoughts (neuro) and language (linguistic) in a systematic way and the scripts that run the life of an individual (programming).

It deals with the understanding and the development of the mind and the entire understanding of the language of the mind in relation to the way it is designed to function and the ways in which it is molded by the personal experiences of an individual. It is simply a study of a person's subjective reality.

A proper understanding of the language of the mind influences every aspect of a person's life from his relationship with others to his communication skills with friends and clients to the general outcome of a person's life. It is a holistic study that puts the spirit, body, past and present of an individual into consideration.

As homo sapiens who are gifted with the ability to think, it is presumed that our most important function is the thought or the thinking function.

NLP, however, brings one to the understanding of the fact that no thought process exists in a vacuum, as they are a product of a person's perspective. It has a presupposition of perception as reality and it holds that the things, we think are colored by the way we think.

For different individuals there are different ways of thinking and interpreting reality. What NLP does is assist in the understanding of these various representational systems to help each person narrow down his own system.

It helps in the understanding of the three different types of thinking patterns which are:

- Visual: deals with both pictures and visual metaphors.

- Auditory: sound (hearing).

- Kinesthetic: deals with the five senses, as well as gut feelings.

In NLP, a person is thought to take absolute control of his mind and ultimately his life. Unlike what is obtainable in psychoanalysis, which places its focus on "why," NLP presents a more practical approach with its focus on the "how."

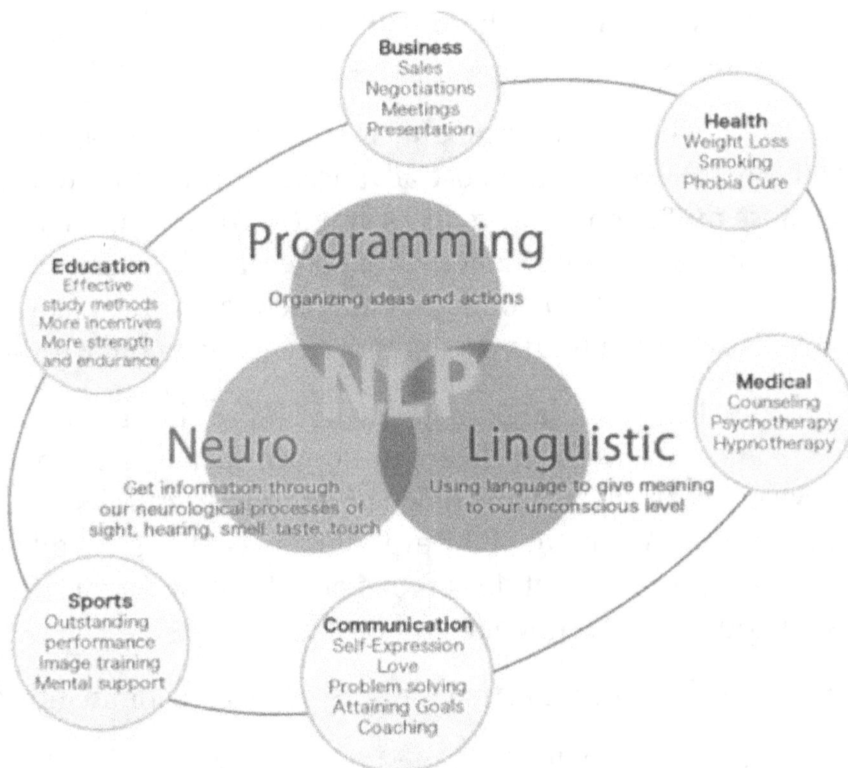


# Verbal and Non-verbal Communication

## How does NLP work?

If you are just coming across this topic for the first time, NLP may appear or seem like magic or hypnosis. When a person is undergoing therapy, this topic digs deep into the unconscious mind of the patient and filters through different layers of beliefs and the person's approach or perception of life to deduce the early childhood experiences that are responsible for a behavioral pattern.

In NLP, it is believed that everyone has the resources that are needed for positive changes in their own lives.

The technique adopted here is meant to help in facilitating these changes.

Usually, when NLP is taught, it is done in a pyramidal structure. However, the most advanced techniques are left for those multi-thousand-dollar seminars. An attempt to explain this complicated subject is to state that the NLPer (as those who use NLP will often call themselves) is always paying keen attention to the person they are working on/with.

Usually, there is a large majority of NLPer that are therapists and they are very likely to be well-meaning people. They achieve their aims by paying attention to those subtle cues like the movement of the eyes, flushing of the skin, dilation of the pupil and subtle nervous tics. It is easy for an NLP user to quickly determine the following:

- The side of the brain that the person uses predominantly.

- The sense (smell, sight, etc.) that is more dominant in a person's brain.

- The way the person's brain stores and makes use of information (the NLPer can deduce all this from the person's eye movement).

- When they are telling a lie or concocting information.

When the NLP user has successfully gathered all this information, they begin to mimic the client in a slow and subtle manner by not only taking on their body language, but also by imitating their speech and mannerisms, so that they begin to talk with the language patterns that are aimed at targeting the primary senses of the client. They will typically fake the social cues that will easily make someone let their guard down so that they become very open and suggestible.

For example, when a person's sense of sight is their most dominant sense, the NLPer will use a language that is very laden with visual metaphors to speak with them. They will say things like: "do you see what I am talking about?" or "why not look at it this way?" For a person that has a more dominant sense of hearing, he will be approached with an auditory language like: "listen to me" or "I can hear where you're coming from."

To create a rapport, the NLPer mirrors the body language and the linguistic patterns of the other person. This rapport is a mental and physiological state which a human being gets into when they lose guard of their social senses. It is done when they begin to feel like the other person who they are conversing with is just like them.

Once the NLPer have achieved this rapport, they will take charge of the interaction by leading it in a mild and subtle manner. Thanks to the fact that they have already mirrored the other person, they will now begin to make some subtle changes in order to gain a certain influence on the behavior of the person. This is also combined with some similar subtle language patterns which lead to questions and a whole phase of some other techniques.

At this point, the NLPer will be able to tweak and twist the person to whichever direction they so desire. This only happens if the other person can't deduce that there is something going on because they assume everything that is occurring is happening organically or that they have given consent to everything.

What this means is that it is quite hard to make use of NLP to get other people to act out of character, but it can be used to get a person to give responses within their normal range of character. This may come in the form of getting them to donate to a charitable cause, or finally making the decision they had been putting off or getting them to go home with you for the night if they had considered it at some point.

At this point, what the NLP user seeks to do may be to either elicit or anchor. When they are eliciting, they make use of both leading and language to get the person to an emotional state of say, sadness. Once they can elicit this state, they can then lead it on with a physical cue by touching the other person's shoulder for example.

According to theory, whenever the NLP user touches the person's shoulder in the same manner, the same emotional state will resurface if they do it again. However, this is only made possible by the successful conditioning of the other person.

When undergoing NLP therapy, it is very possible for the therapist to adopt a content-free approach, which means the therapist can work effectively without taking a critical look at the problem or without even knowing about the problem at all.

This means that there is room for privacy for the client as the therapist does not really need to be told about whichever event took place or whatever issue happened in the past.

Also, prior to the commencement of the therapy, there is an agreement which ensures that the therapist cannot disclose any information, hence the interaction between the therapist and the client remains confidential.

## Is NLP Effective?

In NLP, there is the belief in the need for the perfection of the nature of human creation, so every client is encouraged to recognize the sensitivity of the senses and make use of them in responding to specific problems. As a matter of fact, NLP also holds the belief that it is possible for the mind to find cures to diseases and sicknesses.

The techniques employed by NLP have to do with a noninvasive, medicine-free therapy that enables the client to find out new ways of handling emotional issues such as low self-esteem, lack of confidence, anxiety and destructive relationship patterns. It is also a successful tool in effective bereavement counselling.

With its roots in the field of behavioral science, which was developed by Skinner, Pavlov and Thorndike, NLP makes use of the combination physiology and the unconscious mind to bring about change in the thought process and ultimately the behavior of a person.

# CHAPTER 16

# Hypnosis and Brainwashing

WHAT IS HYPNOSIS? Hypnosis and mind control may seem like the same thing since they involve exerting control over someone else. However, there are glaring contrasts between the two. To recognize the distinctions, it is essential you become more acquainted with what they depend on.

Hypnosis is an artificially induced condition in which the individual reacts to inquiries or prompts from the hypnotist. The procedure can be used on an individual or a gathering of people for a specific reason. At the point when this is utilized for therapeutic purposes, the process is known as hypnotherapy. In any case, when it is being used as a type of diversion for a crowd of people, it tends to be alluded to as organized hypnosis.

Mind control is the way of utilizing a few traps in getting the ideal response you need from others. You can use the secret to get command over what is happening in someone else's psyche.

When it is utilized, it can enable you to center around the subject of your examination.

You can deal with your feelings and contemplations when you participate in this sort of reflection. As a rule, incredible people who accomplished extraordinary achievements in life could have ideal command over their psyches through daily reflection.

It is evident that hypnosis and mind control have clear contrasts. A few components utilized in one may likewise be used in the other, but they are not the same. Everything relies upon how you are ready to draw in the essential standards included.

You have heard of hypnosis. You have surely seen it used on television where the hypnotist tells the person they are getting sleepy. They usually swing some type of pendulum in front of them and then the person falls asleep, completely under the control of the hypnotist. While it happens a bit differently in real life, the end result is the same. Once you can successfully hypnotize people, you can control what they do and think.

Once a person is under hypnosis, you can make suggestions. For example, you want a person to buy you something. You hypnotize them and suggest they buy it for you. Once they come out of the hypnosis, chances are they will get you what you suggested in the very near future.

Now, when you are using hypnosis in this way, you want to do it without the person knowing you are. You will not swing in a pendulum in front of their face to induce the trance state.

# Myths about Hypnosis

Hypnosis is not about making you bark like a dog or cluck like a chicken. It is not about enslaving you under the control of some Svengali who has enraptured you and now will make you do what they want. In truth, hypnosis is about connecting you with your unconscious mind, giving you greater freedom and personal power to transform your life. Every day you experience trance. Whether you are driving home and suddenly look around and do not know how you got home. Alternatively, you sat down in front of the television with Netflix on and suddenly looked up and realized the sun had gone down and you have been sitting there all day.

Maybe you believe that you are bad at math, that you get anxious when something happens, or when your anxious food is a great relaxing thing for you. These are all suggestions and trances that have been embedded into your unconsciousness throughout your life. Hypnotic programming informs in your life, even though you may have never thought you have been hypnotized.

Your brain works on an unconscious and a conscious level. Your consciousness is your gatekeeper; it has a very limited ability to help you make changes, mostly because your conscious mind does not require a lot to get overloaded. It is great in helping you make a decision, on the self-talk that you do, and other such things. But, the very act of you moving your hands requires so many muscles and nerves to fire, so many structural fibers that you, if you were to consciously try to do it, would be impossible. The human foot makes a series of micro-adjustments as a person stands and walks that we have yet been able to replicate in anything and all of that is done in the unconscious.

Your unconscious mind manages almost everything else in your life.

Every second your unconscious brain processes twenty million bits of information, the conscious mind only processes about forty bits of information and that is why hypnosis is so powerful. Our habits, our beliefs, our world outlook, all of these things are embedded in our unconscious mind. How we believe things, why we believe things, how we act on our beliefs, all of these are unconscious. In fact, some studies suggest that even large parts of what feels like conscious decision making happen unconsciously before they happen consciously. Think about that.

What we perceive as a free choice, is oftentimes, a completely unconscious process that we rationalize as a free choice afterward. And to many people, when they hear that, it sounds scary. It might make them even question their view of who they are or what freedoms they have. But to those who understand hypnosis, it offers an opportunity for them to create massive change that they will be able to enjoy and reap the benefits of with ease.

Through hypnosis, a person is often guided into their unconscious and able to layer their desired changes into their unconscious so that they can more easily make changes.

But you might be wondering, you have seen people clucking like a chicken and barking like a dog. You have maybe watched people or heard about people who forgot their name or danced like a stripper. So, what was going on there if hypnosis is just about relaxation, visualization, and mental programming for positive change? Is everyone just pretending? Is it all just fake? Well, the answer is no.

Stage hypnosis relies on people's general ability to want to do crazy things. It uses social pressure and compliance and proper selection to create a compelling display of hypnotic showmanship. The stage hypnotist does a hypnotic test with the audience for anyone that wants to participate and then chooses those who are most responsive. Then when they are on stage, he begins to run them through a series of hypnotic tests, eliminating one person after another who is not fully responding to the hypnotic suggestions that they are putting out there, until all they have on stage is a group of people willing and able to follow directions. And here is the thing, you might have been one of these people, or you have witnessed a friend of yours do it. You might say to yourself that they swear on a stack of bibles that they were hypnotized, and I would say that was 100% true.

The thing is though that what is really happening is that the people on stage have given themselves the permission to be hypnotized and in so doing have abdicated their responsibility to someone else. In 1963 Stanley Milgram wanted to test people's compliance to find out if Nazism was a German weakness, or if people, when faced with authority, could be pushed to do horrible things. Volunteers were told they were doing a study on memory and they were to administer an electric shock to another volunteer if they got the question wrong. At each point, the shocks would increase in intensity. The thing was that everyone except the volunteer was an actor and no one was receiving electric shocks. As they went through the process, a doctor in a white coat would simply insist that they keep going; they keep doing what needs to be done. Each time, people bowed to authority, especially as they were consistently told that the doctor would take full responsibility. Stage hypnosis works in exactly the same way.

They are going along because they can go along because they know that no matter what they do, they have someone they can blame it on. That means they are empowered.

Is hypnosis just a benign thing? The answer here is very mixed. The fact is that hypnosis is a tool, like any other tool, and it can be made a weapon. The thing is that almost nobody knows how to do it and anything you could do in hypnosis to someone, you could do without hypnosis 100x easier. But, of course, hypnosis is powerful. It is after all capable of having you transform your unconscious mind and plant new thoughts, ideas and beliefs inside of it.

Hypnosis is one of the most unique phenomena that only now with the breakthrough technology in brain scans are we even beginning to see any major understanding of. We know now that it transforms the way people think and process information. Where we are usually responding to stimulation (see food and thus want to eat it), instead, when a person has been hypnotized, they act out their thoughts first (meaning if they are on a diet, they do not respond to the food).

This may sound like a small change, but it is not. A powerful transformation makes a person self-directed in their life, given the ability to decide what actions they take, rather than simply being drawn to something form their unconscious programming.

And the best thing about hypnosis is that it is not very difficult to learn. Neither self-hypnosis nor the hypnotic protocols on other people. All of which, you are about to learn.

# Facts about Hypnosis

There are four stages all people go through when you are working to get to their unconscious mind:

1.  You have to make sure that you have their undivided attention.

2.  You have to get them to a state of compliance.

3.  You have to activate their unconscious response.

4.  They are now under your control and you simply need to lead them to the outcome you desire.

# Principal Components of Hypnosis

Hypnosis includes two principal components: acceptance and proposals. Trancelike acceptance is the major proposal conveyed amid the procedure of hypnosis; however, what it should comprise of is a matter of discussion.

Proposals are commonly communicated as suggestions that inspire automatic reactions from the members, who don't trust they have much or any control over the circumstance. A few people are likewise more susceptible than others, and specialists have discovered that these individuals are more likely to have a decreased feeling of authority while under hypnosis.

Susceptibility to hypnosis has been characterized as the capacity to encounter proposed modifications in physiology, sensations, feelings, musings or conduct. Neuroimaging procedures have demonstrated that these individuals show higher activity levels in the prefrontal cortex, foremost cingulate cortex, and parietal systems of the mind amid various periods of hypnosis.

These are regions of the mind associated with a scope of complex capacities, including memory and observation, feelings and assignment learning. Be that as it may, the particular cerebrum components associated with hypnosis are as yet hazy. However, researchers are starting to sort out the neurocognitive profile of this procedure.

How would you know whether somebody has been hypnotized? Various changes indicate that the subject is in a hypnotic trance. NLP calls these profound daze markers, and they are a set of highly detailed observations one can make of the subject. Recognizing such markers requires practice and focus. And not all of these markers need to be present to establish that a subject is under hypnosis.

# CHAPTER 17

# Types of Hypnosis

There are several types of hypnosis that the participant undergoes. Each of them works in a different manner, and some may work to assist in numerous issues. Some types are befitting when it comes to helping the participant to relax while others assist in pain or weight loss management.

Several examples, such as in the case where a certified hypnotherapist or physician is not available, then one may resolve to use the self-hypnosis process. This process takes place when an individual hypnotizes himself, often by means of the method of autosuggestion. The main use of this practice is for self-improvement, and most people would conduct it to quit smoking, or even lower their stress/anxiety levels. While there are, a few people who can self-hypnotize themselves, most individuals find that they require some help in attaining the altered state.

This might include using hypnotic recordings or the mind machine gadgets to aid them to arrive at that state.

The other areas that one can employ self-hypnosis include the overall bodily/physical welfare, to relax, and endure stage fright.

- Traditional Hypnosis

- Ericksonian Hypnosis

- Embedded Technique Neuro-Linguistic Programming (NLP)

- Video Hypnosis

- Subliminal Hypnosis

## What Are the Uses of Hypnosis?

The notion that hypnotherapy can be used to change or alter someone's perception is what makes it a good candidate for a new type of medicinal and therapeutic approach. This alternative approach is used in the United States and Europe to help people with their medical conditions, with their negative habits that impact their health, and even in therapy.

Here are some cases where hypnosis can be useful:

- Helps relieve irritable bowel syndrome (IBS) – Evidence has shown that those who suffer from IBS can benefit from hypnosis to help relieve short-term problems.

- Helps with curing insomnia and sleep disorders – It can be used by counselors and psychologists to help patients manage their insomnia, nightmares, sleep terrors and sleepwalking. In these cases, these specialists will use suggestions in self-control and relaxation to help maintain these conditions.

- Curing migraines – Hypnosis can be used to help treat migraines and tension headaches. The participants that have used it find that it is a great alternative to headache medicine and the side effects that come with taking medicine.

- Pain Control – We are often told that the pain we are feeling is in our head, hypnosis might prove that. It can be used to help those who suffer from clinical pain that they have acquired from surgery and other ailments.

- Quitting Smoking – This is a great way to help those who want to stop with their bad habits, such as smoking, but don't have the will power.

- Weight Control - There is a sense of being able to take control of your life – even on a subconscious level. In this case, the person can be in control of their eating habits and it not being the other way around.

There are three perspective frames that the specialist can use to help change the perspective of the patient.

1. Preframe – Is when the specialist sets the scene before the real event so that the patient sees the real issue.

2. Reframe – This is when the specialist helps change how the patient views the current circumstance or event.

3. Deframe – This is when the specialist changes how the patient views the event by making it irrelevant.

Framing is a great way to help the patient change their behavior because it allows them to get to the core of the problem (the preframe), make them aware of the consequences (the reframe), and then taking away their initial argument because they see it a different way (the deframe).

## Manage Addiction

At this point, the specialist can use hypnosis to help people with addiction manage their problem. They can do this because it helps patients get in touch with their subconscious mind, which is the place where their new suggestions can be planted and continue to grow. Hypnosis can help patients curb their pesky withdrawal symptoms, give them an alternative way to deal with their issues, and give them a drug-free and legal way to escape their problem.

## To Cure Allergies

Studies have shown that hypnosis can help reduce the symptoms of allergies. Using self-hypnosis is psyching yourself out. For instance, if a person who suffers from allergies focuses their thoughts on environments that are allergy-free. They imagine being on a beach with fresh air or on a mountain covered in snow. It can reduce the symptoms they feel because they are telling their mind they are somewhere else.

## Overcome Sexual Dysfunction

Stress can be a huge factor in not being able to perform. Hypnosis helps patients reduce stress and relax when they're in a trance. The specialist will help the patient using techniques such as focused awareness, deep breathing and visualizing things. There can be personal emotional experiences that can cause sexual problems, especially bad experiences. The art of hypnosis can help because it can make the patient relive the experience, release the pain, shame and/or anxiety that it causes, which then helps lead them to have a better and healthier sex life.

## Help with emotional trauma

Emotional trauma can hurt a person in more ways than they are aware of. It can leave people feeling alone, insecure and even helpless in certain situations. Through the use of regression, hypnosis can help manage this problem by having the patient relive the experience again so that they can fully experience the trauma and learn to heal it.

## Help with depression

Traumatic events that the patient might have experienced can be triggers for depression. They can start feeling depressed because someone they loved died, a lot of bad things happened in their lives like a divorce, loss of their home or even their job. The way that hypnosis helps is by having the patient subconsciously deal with the event. They have to face it and discuss what the event is doing that causes them to be depressed. It can take some time because depression can be very severe.

## To overcome and manage OCD/ Anxiety

OCD stands for Obsessive-compulsive disorder, which can be found in your thoughts and your behaviors. Many things can cause OCD. However, the most common reasons are genetics, the result of damaged neural pathways, or as what happens the majority of the time, emotional or developmental issues. Hypnosis works in this case, again, because it goes straight for the subconscious mind where regression is used to take the person back to when they noticed first signs of OCD. This helps them find the root cause, showing them that the reason it started no longer exists.

## Stress management and fighting phobias and fears

Hypnosis is another way to help with these three things that are closely related. The specialist has the patient focusing on their underlying emotions that feed into their stress and keeping it in the front of their mind. Regression can be used here to have the patient find out when stress, in general, started to become the problem.

Once they can find out the reason, they became stressed, or where the fears started, they can start addressing the issue and then realize that those reasons no longer have power over them.

# CHAPTER 18

# Hypnotherapy

WHAT HAPPENS DURING HYPNOTHERAPY? The truth is that hypnosis is a physiological condition that we all practice every day. A few seconds before we sleep and before we wake every morning, we are in a hypnotic trance. Most individuals have undergone what is widely referred to as a 'highway hypnosis,' whereby you climb into the vehicle, continue to travel to a very familiar location like home or work, and are on the way without a strong recollection of your trip.

Some are hypnosis when they participate in an exercise that is exhausting or quite fun, and they realize unexpectedly that they have lost control of time again. This condition is very popular among cyclists, musicians, joggers, athletes of high achievement, and people who participate actively in behaviors that involve intense attention and concentrate at times in conjunction with repeated movements.

This is only necessary for someone to be hypnotized because they choose which another essential part of the hypnotic process is. At no point should someone be compelled to partake in any behavior they consider socially or ethically disgusting? Someone retains a sense of right and wrong in hypnotization, and the basic self is very present. Sometimes in a series of a performer who plays and making participants do crazy actions to their crowd, a screening procedure has taken place through which the hypnotist secretly tests the suddenness and ability of applicants across varying stages of experience so long that the only people remaining on stage are the most suggestible ones, i.e.

That explains so many hypnotics and hypnotherapists claim that all hypnosis explains 'self-hypnosis' because the basic truth remains that you won't succeed because you wish it to happen. It's just that easy, because why does anybody choose to be hypnotized if it's a normal condition first and if the hypnotist or hypnotherapist cannot transform the mind immediately?

The solution is pretty straightforward, but first of all, we feel joy in hypnosis. Yeah, it feels nice to be hypnotized. Hypnosis can only be calculated by looking at brain waves, so we believe that the more reliable, weaker brain waves we refer to as brain waves alpha or theta are linked to the decreased development of 'feel nice' neurotransmitters, including serotonin so dopamine in the brain and endorphins throughout the body. Hypnosis creates feelings of peace, comfort, and enjoyment in the body. Hypnosis happens while our brain waves report in the low alpha and theta scale, reaching all the neurotransmitters "feel nice." By the way, brain wave rhythms for regular physical life are called beta and brain waves for the night. Such findings are objectively observable and have been confirmed time and over again through valid empirical methods. Do remember that every person has a distinct and unique experience with hypnosis, from feeling as though they had fallen asleep to noticing some subtle improvements in themselves to wondering how hypnosis was accomplished in all that was between them. The crucial thing that should be noted is that the aid of a professional hypnotist or hypnotherapist is required with a degree of hypnosis, such that the calming results of such neurotransmitters are noticed, and some effective research is begun. This being said, others tend to practice self-hypnosis methods without assisting any individual in achieving successful results themselves.

Often essential to remember is that we have a clear exposure to the subconscious mind while hypnosis is taking effect. The subconscious mind becomes like a hard disk on a computer; it knows what has occurred in your life, has organized and stored all the required details for everyday activity, tracks the body's reflexes and actions, and stores knowledge at a pace of four billion bits per second!

Through hypnosis, we are able to get through the normal filtrating mechanism that occurs between the conscious mind and subconscious mind to have a clear exposure to the vast store of experiences, feelings, perceptions, concepts and other knowledge in the subconscious mind to help discover what can impede the recovery, the thinking, the development or the displacement of old-fashioned beliefs, unhealing. It's not a lack of control, as others may say, hypnosis is, in essence, a mechanism of taping into inherent energy already present in the subconscious mind! It is not a loss of control.

It makes it much simpler for constructive ideas about improvement in the subconscious mind to be implemented such that successful outcomes of an active life can be made. Clearly stated, we know better, we know quicker and more effectively because of the easy exposure to the subconscious mind.

Of reality, children between the ages of six and seven are under regular hypnosis very often because of the tremendous amount of learning that happens at that period with respect to motor skills, vocabulary, attitudes, cultural and social norms, and so on. This method has little at all to do with intellect. Many questioners assume that only the feeble mind can be hypnotized, although, in reality, hypnosis can be readily done for those who are willing to focus, concentrate, and care. In addition, hypnosis should be utilized as a method for attention and performance enhancement in the absence of ADD and ADHD.

This is a normal state that we are both able to experience every day, that we feel good and, ultimately, that hypnosis can be a secure, useful resource to gain greater consciousness, to develop better self-control and to reach the wisdom contained inside the subconscious mind, which otherwise will not be accessible to the conscious mind in for recovery, development and social improvement reasons. Is Hypnotherapy Effective?

# To Succeed in Your Hypnosis

### 1. Design a favorable plan

Designing a plan of action does not mean that you make

complex arrangements on how-to carry-on conversation with your subject. Rather, it means that you do some groundwork so that you know what generally works in trying to work someone into a trance and what doesn't work. You need, for instance, to have a good range of effective words and phrases that you can apply in communication in order to effectively write your ideas onto the person's mind.

And do not behave in stereotype when it comes to body language, your choice phrases and how you generally handle yourself when relating to that person. If you make this mistake, you may either look ridiculous or put off your subject. Yet your intention is to lure the person into trusting you so that you can both have good rapport. And although it helps better if you can get some personal details about your subject in advance, when it comes to planning for the hypnosis process, make a plan that is flexible; one that can you can use with almost anyone.

## 2. Read your subject's emotional state

Do you think you can make headway trying to hypnotize someone who is in rage or one who is suspicious of people around? It just cannot work. For one they may not even pay attention to what you are saying. That is why it is important that you be observant and try to assess how the person is generally feeling, even before you begin your hypnosis. If you sense some tension, try and establish what is causing it. If the person is upset, find out the cause. And the reason you are trying to establish the person's emotional state is so that you can help them relax and feel at home within the environment you are in.

Remember we mentioned earlier on that you can tell that your subject is ready to get into a trance when their pause is stable, and their breathing is regular. In short, a relaxed state is conducive for transitioning into a trance.

## 3. Assess the effect of your plan beforehand

You don't have to wait till you have a conversation with your subject for you to have an idea how the person is going to respond. For one, there is room to play the scene in your mind. Again, you have room to assess the person's mood, demeanor and attitude as you begin to make them at ease with conversation. Something else you cannot also afford to miss includes the person's eye movements. The minute you notice your subject's eye movements begin to sway from side to side, you know time is ripe for hypnosis.

# CHAPTER 19

# Understand That Hypnotherapy Has Its Limitations

YOU ARE CONSIDERING SORTING OUT a problem by paying a visit to a hypnotherapist. Before you do, I suggest that you mull over a few things about the responsibilities of that hypnotherapist, as well as some of the realities of hypnotherapy itself. After all, you want to go in for therapy with realistic expectations and a clear understanding of what to expect from your therapist and the process itself. The information here gives you just that.

The truth is that hypnotherapy is not magic and hypnotherapists do not have special powers. You're not going to walk in for a hypnotherapy session and walk out an hour more with all your cares and woes miraculously cured, hallelujah!

Many myths surround hypnotherapy and many people walk into a session expecting the impossible. When you go for therapy, enter into it with realistic expectations. That means understanding what can be done and what can't be done. It can be a great help to you in the long run.

Cure is a word often misused by patients and by some hypnotherapists. Cure implies that something is going to go away. Possibly for good and never come back. Oh, how I wish therapy were that simple. Unfortunately, it isn't, and it never will be. No hypnotherapist worth his or her salt will promise a cure to his or her patients because he or she cannot guarantee that the problem you work on will go away. It may; or you may learn to live more comfortably with it; or it may go away and return in the future; or it may be that nothing changes at all. All these possible outcomes apply to any form of therapy or medical procedure. You may be thinking 'What's the point in going for therapy then, if there's no guarantee of change?' The fact of the matter is that no therapy can guarantee change. However, hypnotherapy does have an excellent track record and the evidence shows it to be very effective at helping people to make positive changes to their lives and to achieve their goals.

Hypnotherapy helps. That means it is an aid to overcoming something, and as such, relies on the effort you are prepared to put into the therapy process. It can't do it all on its own. You Must Learn To Accept The Limitations Of Hypnotherapy

When you go for your hypnotherapy session you need to be realistic about what it can achieve. Although hypnotherapy's effects are wide-ranging, like any other therapy approach it does have its limitations. As with anything and everything, many factors determine the outcome of hypnotherapy.

# Such Factors Include the Following Elements

## Your Symptom

Hypnotherapy can help resolve many different symptoms. However, it cannot help with everything. Future topics in this manuscript will give you a good idea as to the type of symptoms that can and can't benefit from hypnotherapy. For example, cigarette addiction can be treated, whereas the treatment of heroin addiction should be left to the medical profession. If in doubt, ask your therapist if hypnotherapy is right for your symptom.

Your symptom itself often determines the length of time you spend in therapy. Smoking cessation can take as little as one session to complete. However, if you are being treated for something more involved, such as bulimia, you can expect a longer course of treatment because of the deeper issues involved with this condition and its treatment.

## Your Expectations

Are you expecting too much from hypnotherapy? Do you think it is a magical panacea that will get rid of your symptom at the click of a finger?

The 'I want to lose two stone by Friday' mindset is doomed to failure. Your expectations must be realistic from the outset. Hypnotherapy is therapy, not magic! Discuss your expectations with your therapist and be prepared to have the reality of the process pointed out to you.

So what can you realistically expect from hypnotherapy? You can expect to have a very good chance at relieving your symptom. As with any course of treatment, medical or not, you can't have an absolute guarantee that the treatment will work. Why? Because of the factors we discuss here.

You can also expect to put some effort into your therapy process by carrying out homework assignments that continue the therapy process, even when you are not with your therapist. You can also expect that your therapist will put in as much time and effort as is needed to help you overcome your symptom.

## Your Fears

Are you at ease with your hypnotherapy session? Do you fear anything about the process you're going through, such as whether the effects of your therapy will be long-lasting, or just how effective it will be? Perhaps you're worried that you aren't going into trance in the way that you thought you would. Maybe you're concerned that being in trance now will affect you during the meeting you're chairing for the day.

If these or any other fears spring to mind during your therapy session, discuss them with your therapist before, during – yes, you can talk in trance – or after the trance has concluded, and let her put your mind at ease. Letting such fears fester away without discussing them interferes with your chances of having a good outcome for your therapy.

## Your Relationship With The Hypnotherapist

Is it a good one? Do you feel comfortable with her? Is your therapist someone you can work with? Like any relationship, the better it is, the smoother things run. If you don't feel comfortable with, or dislike, your therapist for any reason, the all-important trust factor will not be there. If you don't trust your therapist then your mind won't trust the therapy process itself. If this is the case, then politely say 'Thanks, but no thanks' to your therapist, and find another in whose company you do feel comfortable. Remember, the therapy sessions are for you, not your therapist.

What's going on in your life at the moment: Life has its ups and downs and these may help or hinder your therapy. If all is hunky-dory and good things are happening in your life, you tend to feel upbeat, positive, and motivated – you have what's known as a positive mindset. These good feelings affect the way you view the course of your therapy, making you more optimistic, positive, and motivated about the whole process and its outcome. With this positive mindset you could very well find that your unconscious mind is more open to the suggestions your hypnotherapist is giving; speeding up the process of change.

# CHAPTER 20

# The Autohypnosis: Exercise

THE SECRET IS THAT EVERY HYPNOTIST NEEDS to have a personal experience with hypnosis. The best hypnotists go into hypnosis while working with clients.

You may have already had a personal experience with hypnosis, and that's why you're interested in pursuing this profession. Or perhaps you had a loved one who experienced hypnosis. Or you're curious about how the heart and mind work and have looked at other related techniques such as flow state or meditation.

For my students, the personal experience with hypnosis is often related to overcoming a lack of confidence in business or hypnosis skills and mastery. You don't need any advanced skills now; you'll learn them. You simply need a big heart, desire to serve, and the courage to help people do things they've never been able to do – starting with yourself.

Hypnosis can occur with or without the person's knowledge. If a person knows they are being hypnotized, they may be more aware of what is going on, but they are still susceptible to manipulation.

Hypnosis is a technique which alters a person's state of consciousness in order to make them highly suggestible to behaviors which they would not normally exhibit. It has been used historically in everything from parlor shows to intense psychotherapy and is subject to a great deal of skepticism. In the realm of dark psychology, hypnosis could be used to cause the subject to act on another's behalf or otherwise behave in a way abhorrent to their normal state of being. Because people in a state of hypnosis are often hyper-focused on the task they've been given, they are driven to complete that task no matter the consequence.

Hypnosis is used for many different reasons, and it can be used for positive change as well as negative change. Hypnosis has several elements, and they may or may not be present in different iterations of the hypnosis process. It starts with an induction. Remember in cartoons, when they have the illustration of the swirling visual effect, and some head-wrapped mystic is holding a watch with the swirl in front of a person's face? This cartoon depiction is what is known formally as the induction process.

The induction process is when a person is actually trying to change another person's state of consciousness. In order to make the person more suggestible and influence-able, hypnosis uses an actual transformation of the state of consciousness. In order to think about this, you can think about a person who is typical and awake, a person who is paralyzed but otherwise capable, and a person who is in a coma.

There are many gradations to the state of consciousness that a person is in. The person who is being hypnotized is not paralyzed, but they are closer to that than normal consciousness. Normal consciousness allows the person to have too much stability and defenses. The state that is induced in hypnosis is one where a person does not have all their defenses in play.

After the induction process has been successfully implemented, then the person can be told what to do or what to think. Since the person who is being hypnotized has their defenses uncovered and weakened, they are able to take instructions without question.

One method that works in NLP as a tool for hypnosis is anchoring. Anchoring is when a hypnotist uses something very familiar to you to bring you to that induction space where you are very suggestible. It might be a nursery rhyme, it might be a name you were called when you were younger, or it might be a song. This works to engage your subconscious, and it tricks you into thinking you are safe and allowed to be engaged in the suggestions.

Another NLP –based method for hypnosis is the NLP Flash. The flash works by switching the reward to punishment, or the punishment to a reward. So, if there is something that you like to do which you are trying to stop doing, like smoking cigarettes, the hypnotist will make you think about a cigarette, and then they will make you experience something very uncomfortable, like an electric shock or some other kind of physical or emotional pain. This is a very dark method and can have very deep implications.

Hypnotism can be a very strong way to persuade someone against their will. It may not be as secretive as the other methods of persuasion, but it can be used without your knowledge.

# Brainwashing

## What is Brainwashing?

Brainwashing here will be tackled in terms of its use in psychology. In this relation, brainwashing is described as a technique of idea reform through social impact. This type of social influence is happening during the day to everyone, regardless of whether they recognize it or not. Social impact is the collection of methods that are used to change other people's behaviors, attitudes, and beliefs. For example, compliance methods that are used in the office might technically be thought about a form of brainwashing because they need you to act, and when you are doing the job, you feel a specific way.

Brainwashing can end up being more of a social problem in severe form because these methods work at changing the way somebody thinks without the subject's approval.

For persuading to work effectively, the subject is going to go through total seclusion and dependency because of its intrusive impact on the subject. This is one of the reasons that some of the brainwashing cases that are understood, happen in totalistic cults or jail camps. The brainwasher, or the agent, need to gain complete control.

The method of brainwashing is still up for dispute, whether it will work. A lot of psychologists hold the belief that it is possible to brainwash somebody as long as the right conditions are present. Even then, the entire process is not as extreme as it is presented in the media. There are likewise different meanings of brainwashing that make it harder to figure out the effects of brainwashing on the subject. A few of these meanings needs to be some threat to the physical body of the subject, to consider brainwashing. Even the practices done by lots of extremist cults would not be regarded as fact brainwashing as no physical abuse happens if you follow this definition.

Other definitions of brainwashing will count on control and browbeating without physical force to get the change in the beliefs of the subjects. In any case, experts think that the effect of brainwashing, even under the perfect conditions, is just a brief term occurrence. They believe that the old personality of the subject is not removed with the practice; instead, it is put into hiding and will return when the new personality is not strengthened anymore.

Robert Jay Lifton created some intriguing ideas on brainwashing in the 1950s after he studied detainees of the Chinese and Korean War camps. During his observations, he identified.

This process started with attacks on the sense of self with the prisoner and then ended with an expected change in beliefs of the subject.

There are some steps that Lifton defined for the brainwashing process in the subjects that he studied.

1.  An attack on the personality of the subject

2.  Requiring regret on the subject

3.  Forcing the subject into self-betrayal

4.  Reaching a breaking point

5.  Providing the subject leniency if they change.

6.  Funneling the guilt in the intended direction

7.  Launching the subject of supposed guilt

8.  Progressing to consistency

This indicates that all of the normal social references that the subject is used to coming in contact with are not available. Also, mind clouding strategies will be used to accelerate the procedure, such as poor nutrition and sleep deprivation.

Be real of all brainwashing cases; typically there is a presence of some physical damage, which contributes to the target having problems in thinking independently and seriously like they usually would.

During the practice of brainwashing, the subject will be persuaded to change their beliefs about something through a combination of various techniques. As the subject absorbs this new info, they will be rewarded for expressing concepts and thoughts which go along with these originalities. The fulfilling is what will be used to strengthen the brainwashing that is happening.

# The History and Future of Brainwashing

## Brainwashing Today

Brainwashing is not new to the society. People have been using these methods for a very long time. For example, in a historical context, those who were detainees of wars were typically broken down before being encouraged to changes sides. Some of the most compelling cases of these would result in the detainee becoming an impassioned change to the new team. These practices were new at the beginning and would typically be implemented depending on who supervised. Over time, regard to brainwashing was established, and some more methods were presented to make the practice more universal. The newer strategies would depend on the field of psychology because many of those ideas were used to show how people might change their minds through persuasion.

The subject can be around other people and affects, they will find out how to think as a person, and the brainwashing will not work at all.

## Challenges of Brainwashing in the Future

The entire process of brainwashing can take some months to even years. It is not something that is going to happen in merely a conversation, and for some parts, it will not be able to occur beyond jail camps and a couple of separated cases. For some parts, those who undergo brainwashing have done so when someone is simply attempting to convince them of a new perspective.

# CHAPTER 21

# The Deception

T HE GOING WITH KIND OF MIND CONTROL that will be investigated is deception. This mind control technique will have two or three likenesses to control in the way those controllers will use a great deal of deception so as to locate a functional pace objective.

This fragment will go into more bits of information concerning how deception functions, the methodologies related with it, and a piece of the examination that has been found.

## What is Deception?

In any case is the definition about what deception is. Deception, alongside subterfuge, confusion, imagines, misleading, and beguilement, is a show used by the position to spread emotions in the subject about things that are contortions, or which are basically almost the whole way feelings. Deception can consolidate a collection of things, for example, disguise, and spread, impedance, capable deception, presentation, and dissimulation. The director will have the decision to control the cerebrum of the subject considering the way that the subject will trust in them. The subject will recognize what the ace is communicating and may even be basing reachable plans and forming their reality dependent on the things that the expert has been letting them know.

On the off chance that the master is rehearsing the methodology of deception, the things they have been telling the subject will be counterfeit. Trust can without a considerable amount of a stretch be pummeled once the subject discovers, which is the clarification the ace must be gifted at the technique of deception and exceptional at getting something moving if they need to proceed with their subject.

Typically, deception will come up the degree that affiliations and it can incite sentiments of vulnerability and unfaithfulness between the two partners who are in the relationship. This is considering the way that deception hurts the rules of most affiliations and is in like way observed to impact the needs that go with that relationship. Considerable number people need to have the choice to have a real discussion with their embellishment; if they have discovered that their partner is surprising, they would need to understand how to use confusion and impedance to get the solid and reasonable data that they need. The trust would in like way be gone from the relationship, making it difficult to develop the relationship back to where it had once been.

The subject would dependably be exploring the things that the ace was outlining for them, thinking about whether the story was authentic, or something made up. Because of this new vulnerability, most affiliations will end once the subject finds a couple of arrangements concerning the deception of the master.

# Types of Deception

Deception is a sort of correspondence that depends upon oversights and lies so as to persuade the subject of the world that best fits the ace. Since there is correspondence required, there will in like way be a few specific sorts of deception that could be happening. As appeared by the Interpersonal Deception Theory, there are 5 undeniable sorts of deception that are found.

A piece of these have been appeared in different sorts of mind control, displaying that there can be some covering. The five basic sorts of deception include:

1.  **Deceptions**

This is the place the overseer makes up data or gives data that is by no means equal to what is reality. They will demonstrate this data to the subject as truth and the subject will consider it to be reality. This can be risky since the subject won't grasp that they are being proceeded with sham data; if the subject comprehended the data was false, they would not likely be talking with the power and no deception would happen.

## 2.   Avoidances

This is the place the head will make negating, crude, or degenerate clarifications. This is done to lead the subject to get disordered and to not get a handle on what's happening. It can correspondingly assist the head with disguising any trace of disappointment if the subject returns in the future and tries to reprimand them for the phony data.

## 3.   Mask

This is one of the most for the most part saw sorts of deception that are used. Masks are the place the manager disregards data that is material or essential to the specific condition, deliberately, or they look into any immediate that would cover data that is fitting to the subject for that specific setting. The chairman won't have truly misdirected the subject; anyway, they will have ensured that the basic data that is required never makes it to the subject.

## 4.   Bending

This is the place the director will exaggerate a reality or distort a touch to turn the story the way wherein that they may require. While the authority may not be truly deceptive the subject, they are going to cause the circumstance to appear as though a more conspicuous strategy than it truly is, or they may change reality a piece with the target that the subject will do what they need.

## 5.   Under-depictions

A modest depiction of the truth is the exact opposite of the paltriness device in that the head will make light of or constrain bits of this present reality. They will tell the subject that an occasion isn't that goliath obviously of activity when in truth it could be what picks whether the subject finds the opportunity to graduate or gets that colossal progress. The ace will have the choice to return in the future and say how they didn't perceive how epic of a strategy it was, leaving them to look amazing and the subject to search in every way that really matters irrelevant on the off chance that they fight.

These are only a couple of the sorts of deception that may be found. The star of deception will use any procedure that is open to them to locate a useful pace objective, much like what happens in different sorts of mind control. If they can appear at their objective using another methodology against the subject, by then they will do it so the rundown above isn't the littlest piece specific. The chairman of deception can be staggeringly perilous because the subject won't have the choice to admit all with what is and what a demonstration of deception is; the star will be so talented at what they do that it will be essentially difficult to comprehend what is reality and what isn't.

# Reasons for Deception

### Detecting Deception

While it might be difficult to comprehend which components show when deception is going on, there are a few causes that are customary of deception. Reliably the subject won't understand that these parts have happened except for if the director has lied or been trapped in the show of misdirecting. These are parts that will be seen in the future if the director is using the arrangement of deception in the correct manner. The three principle bits of deception join cover, disguise, and reenactment.

## Cover

The significant bit of deception is disguise. This is the place the director is trying to cover reality in another manner with the target that the subject won't appreciate that they are feeling the loss of the data. From time to time this strategy will be used when the chairman uses misleading explanations when they are telling data. The subject won't understand that the disguising has happened until in eventually when these certainties are uncovered as it were. The ace will be gifted in covering reality with the target that it is staggeringly difficult for the subject to locate a couple of arrangements concerning the deception by some accidental occasion.

## Disguise

Disguise is another part that can be found during the time spent deception. When this occurs, the administrator is endeavoring to establish a connection of being some other individual or thing. This is when the authority is hiding something imperative to them from the subject, for example, their certifiable name, what they achieve for an employment, who they have been with, and what they are up to when they go out. This goes more distant than basically changing the outfit that somebody wears in a play or a film; when disguise is used during the time spent deception, the administrator is endeavoring to change their whole persona in order to delude and deceive the subject.

There are a couple of examples that can outline the use of disguise during the time spent deception. The first is in a long time to the master covering themselves, generally as another person, so they are not indisputable. The administrator may do this in order to get by and by into a crowd of people that couldn't care less for them, change their characters to make somebody like them, or for another inspiration to propel their destinations. Once in a while, the word disguise can insinuate the administrator covering the certified thought of a suggestion with desires for hiding an effect or motivation that is detested with that recommendation. Every now and again this sort of disguise is found in proclamation or political turn.

Disguise can be hazardous because it is hiding the authentic thought of what's going on. In case the master is covering who they are from the subject, it might be very difficult for the subject to figure out who they genuinely are. When information is held from the subject, it fogs how they can think since they don't have the right information to choose reasonable choices. While the subject may feel that they are choosing astute choices readily, the master has expelled key information that may change the subject's point of view.

## Reenactment

The third piece of deception is known as reenactment. This involves indicating the subject information which is counterfeit. There are three systems that can be used in reenactment including interference, production, and mimicry. In mimicry, or the recreating of another model, the pro will be unwittingly depicting something that resembles them. They may have an idea that resembles someone else's and instead of giving credit; they will say that it is all theirs. This kind of reenactment can much of the time occur through sound-related, visual, and different techniques.

Assembling is another device that the administrator may use when using deception.

This implies the administrator will take something that is found when in doubt and change it with the objective that it is exceptional.

They may describe to a story that didn't happen or incorporate embellishments that intensify it sound best or over it really was. While the focal point of the story may be legitimate, yes they got an awful assessment on a test, it will have some extra things put in, and for example, the educator gave them a terrible assessment purposely. In reality the administrator didn't contemplate and that is the explanation they got the horrible assessment regardless.

Finally, interference is another kind of amusement in deception. This is when the administrator endeavors to get the subject to focus on a choice that is other than the real world; generally by prodding or offering something that might be more luring than reality that is being covered up. For example, if the spouse is cheating and thinks the wife is starting to discover, he may bring home a valuable stone ring to redirect her from the issue for a brief time span. The issue with this framework is that it every now and again doesn't prop up long and the master must discover another way to deal with mislead the subject in order to prop the methodology up.

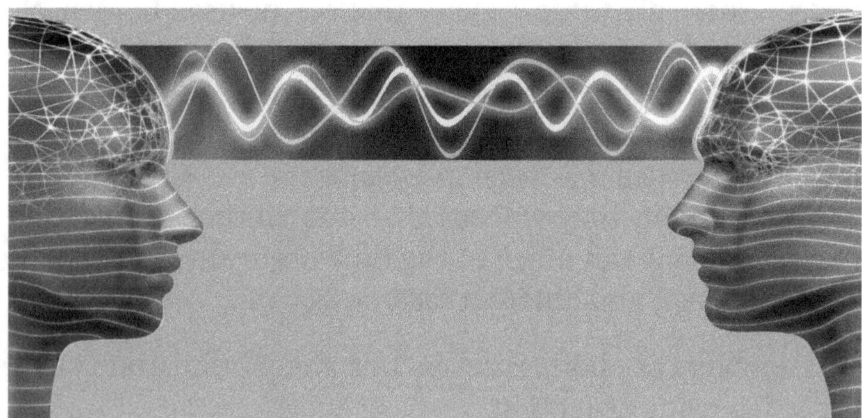

# CHAPTER 22

# How to Protect Yourself Against Emotional Predators

EMOTIONAL PSYCHOLOGY AS A NECESSARY ingredient for success. While mind control can help in some situations, having natural influence can be better in many instances. Influence is much more subtle and often non-verbal. Heck, just by having influence, you'll be grouped in with other players in the big leagues. After all, influence is not just an advantage; it's a necessity for most leaders and persuaders.

The charisma, charm, and expertise displayed through influence are associated with top tier qualities. But how do you achieve it?

# Methods of Influencing Individuals

There are more methods of influencing another human being than one might be aware of. One proven method is that of mirroring or copying the behavior of another person. This takes the form of a type of body language in reverse. Instead of using your body to convey a message, you use their body language and play it back to them. By using the same motions, head positions and similar facial expressions, it has been proven that you can create a more harmonious relationship with another person. Obviously, this makes that person more vulnerable to you being able to influence her, and this may be advantageous if you need to persuade that person to take a particular course of action.

The problem with mirroring, as it is referred to, is that if the other person detects you are doing it then it has the opposite effect to that which was intended, and you can lose influence altogether. If you feel this is a tactic that may be useful to you, and I don't want to persuade you here, then you must be at your most discreet. The perception that they are being copied will lead people to conclude that you are mocking them.

Another method that uses a somewhat similar strategy is that of social proof. In other words, if everyone else is doing something then you should too. The fashion industry has traded on this since it began. It is not for no reason that we find that fashion follows trends from year to year. Few people like, or can tolerate, being the odd one out. If straight hair and tight jeans are in this year, then nearly everyone will be wearing their hair straight with tight jeans. Of course, all you need to do to really reiterate your marketing position is get a well-known celebrity to wear tight jeans and straighten their hair, and you are away. This phobia of breaking the chain of peer acceptance is very powerful. That is why many advertisements use expressions like "nine out of ten customers found that such and such a product worked wonders for their health".

Immediately they have established that this is the thing that most people are doing and the fear of being seen as out of place will kick in automatically. Creating a crowd mentality of one kind or another is an almost guaranteed method of persuading people in a particular direction. It is a method that has been used by politicians, dictators, and religious promulgators, almost since those professions came into existence. Once you grasp how this very basic human characteristic works and how widespread it is, then you are able to capitalize on it. If you wish to persuade a child to do something, then, first of all, you should convince that child that all his friends are doing the same thing. This simple technique relates to the workplace as much as it does to the playground.

Probably some of the most adept people at persuasion are politicians, and they love to use this strategy to persuade others.

Unfortunately, they are weak when it comes to recognizing when this method is being used against them, and that is why you will so often see politicians changing their point of view if they feel that there is a majority going the other way. We need to be aware of this and make sure that our own paths are not influenced by group pressure. As stated earlier, our integrity is an important factor in maintaining influence, and this may evaporate if we are perceived to sway too much in the direction of the crowd.

Tests have also proven that our influence on others is increased dramatically if we are perceived to be an authority in a certain area. Having recognized qualifications displayed on the wall of an office has been shown to increase the authority that a person is perceived to have. It goes much further, though. If somebody describes you as an authority on a certain subject, then your status will be elevated, and your persuasiveness increases. It has even been shown that even if the third party promoting your expertise is somebody you know well, the mere fact that they speak highly of you will influence the other person's perception of you. Advertising agencies like to use a doctor or dentist to promote medical or dental products as many people will believe that their endorsement proves the product is effective. Often these medical professionals are nothing other than actors with white coats on. Hopefully, you won't need to stoop to that level, but if you can persuade someone to put in a good word for you, it may not be a bad idea. As people come to accept you as an authority in one area, they will be ready to accept you as an authority in other areas.

Influencing others is also a matter of being able to pick out other key influencers in a group and harness their power.

If you are working with a group of people, it's a waste of time to try persuading one of the less influential members of something if they are only going to be swayed by someone else, coming along with a contrary line of thought. Instead, you need to focus your efforts on the most influential people in the knowledge that if you can win them over to your idea, then the battle is half won.

Now when it comes to influencing people, most of us tend to make the same mistakes. We underestimate ourselves and don't work towards it.

As we've just mentioned, you can cosmetically seem influential by placing your qualifications in your office for everyone to see, but cosmetic influence can only get you so far. In high stake, public situations, influence comes from your network. Who you know and how well. That's why you'll see everyone from politicians to CEOs name dropping people they know in obvious or subtle fashions. If you have correspondence with someone such as Tim Cook, as someone who works in the software or tech industry, your credibility and influence have double the effect. This is often overlooked or considered as a secondary, automatic response to gaining influence. However, if you use your intent to gain this type of influence early, you'll establish yourself as an experienced persuader early on.

That said, it's not every day Tim Cook, or other such high-ranking individuals are available to connect with. Or are they? One of the best-kept secrets by expert persuaders is their ability to connect with others. Their networking tactics are often not talked about since that's how they derive a large chunk of their influence. That said, their tactic is very simple and doable. You simply ask.

In the age of social media, most influencers are looking to connect and build their networks. They're just waiting for brave, worthy persuaders to contact them. For them, your connection is a valuable way to get their word out there and reinforce themselves as authority figures in their respective fields. For you, it's your ticket to getting one of the easiest credibility boosts.

It may not seem easy or natural the first few times you connect, but you'll soon see how easy it is to connect with influencers around the globe. Just start with a hello and a free valuable offer and take things from there.

There are a few things you should keep in mind, however. Some dos and don'ts when it comes to influencing people. After all, if your employees, friends or loved ones notice how you're trying to control them in any fashion, it might prove to be troublesome, at best.

# The secrets to influencing people the right way

## 1. Ask for influence

No one is going to hand you influence on a silver platter, or any platter for that matter. You need to proactively achieve it. Networking is the most beneficial skill you can pick up. It not only gains you influence but helps give you access to expert, established persuaders and learn from them. If you're too scared to ask for influence, no one will consider you worthy enough to possess it.

## 2. Don't say no

No is a negative word in most situations, particularly when

it comes to persuading people. While most of us can recognize opportunities and say yes to those, most don't realize how they might be saying no to someone else. Through our negativity, we can be answering for the person. So, as you've learned earlier, keep your message positive and always lean towards yes.

### 3. Don't influence strangers

Influencing partly works because of a connection between two or more people. Others need to trust your words and empathize with you in order to get influenced by you. That's why you see a lot of big religious evangelicals and motivational speakers form a connection with their audience before diving into their teachings. The first step should always involve friendship and a genuine one at that. As said, you're not trying to manipulate people, so don't give anyone the impression that you're trying to use them.

### 4. Listen to what others have to say

If you're not paying attention, it's unlikely you'll leave a good impression on anyone, especially when you're dealing with the big dogs. To show you're listening, ask related questions and stay involved in the conversation.

### 5. Don't talk about yourself

This is one of the biggest mistakes rising persuaders make. Making a conversation or situation about yourself isn't in line with persuasion, but borders on manipulation. Not to mention, it becomes a major turn off. Only talk about yourself as much as the other person directs.

Once you start applying these simple tricks, you'll notice a dramatic change in how people, big or small, treat you.

Blending different types of influences according to your strengths is how you make yourself a credible persuader.

# Simple Advice for Dealing with Other People

- It is good to avoid arguments. This is the way to obtain the most from it.

- Make others aspire for a nobler, higher motives.

- Begin in a friendly manner and act in a friendly way.

- Show respect for the other person and other person's opinions. Never judge or condemn them.

- In case that you are wrong, admit is simply, quickly and emphatically.

- Let the other person do the talking. Be a good listener.

- Let the other person think that it is she or he who have brought forth a new idea.

- Try to be empathetic. Put yourself in the perspective of another person.

- Sympathize with the other person's thoughts, feelings, and desires.

- Be charming in presenting your ideas.

- Be challenging.

# CHAPTER 23

# Practical Tips for Dealing with Predators

Y OU CAN COME ACROSS MANIPULATORS in all aspects of your life, both professional and personal. Whether you want to believe it or not, even those you love the most and hold dear can be manipulators. You might have to deal with manipulative partners, manipulative parents, or even manipulative coworkers. Regardless of the manipulator, you are dealing with; you can use the tips given here to deal with manipulation and manipulative people.

It isn't always easy, but you must learn to do so. After all, you are the only one who is responsible for your overall well-being.

# Basic Fundamental Rights

A fundamental right is inalienable, and no one can take it away from you. This is one thing you must keep in mind whenever you come across any person who is a psychological manipulator. You must not only recognize your rights but must also prevent the violation of these rights. As long as you don't harm others, you must stand up for yourself and protect your rights at all costs. If you knowingly harm someone, you may lose some of these fundamental rights. Here are a couple of basic human rights you must be aware of.

- You have the right to be treated with dignity and respect.

- You are free to express your opinions, feelings, desires, and wants.

- You are free to set your priorities, and no one can force you to do something.

- You don't have to feel guilty when you say "no."

- You have the right to set specific boundaries for yourself.

- You have the right to have different opinions, and you don't have to agree with everyone.

- You not only have a right, but an obligation to safeguard yourself mentally, emotionally, and physically.

All these fundamental rights define your boundaries. You must not only enforce your limitations on others but must also respect them yourself. Of course, you'll come across people who don't respect your rights. Especially those who resort to psychological manipulation, strive to deprive others of their rights so that they can exert control over you. However, keep in mind, you have the power to decide what you want to do, and you are the only one in charge of your life.

## Maintain Some Distance

A manipulator often puts up a façade for the world to see and doesn't let his true intentions rise to the surface. A simple way to detect or spot a manipulator is to see the way he acts in front of different people and various situations. Most of us tend to exhibit social differentiation to a certain degree; emotional predators and psychological manipulators tend to dwell on the extreme ends of the spectrum. An emotional manipulator can be extremely polite one instant and unnervingly hostile eventually. If you notice this kind of behavior from anyone in your circle, maintain your distance. If you cannot get away from such a person or avoid social interactions, then limit your interactions. Spend as little time dealing with such a person as possible. Even being around them will hurt you in ways you cannot begin to comprehend. You don't have to worry about being responsible for their feelings. If the manipulator tries to make you feel guilty for maintaining your distance, it is a part of his manipulative nature, and you're not obligated to fix them. So, stay away.

## No Personalization

A manipulator is continuously going to look for your weaknesses, and once he understands them, he will exploit them.

Therefore, he might try to make you feel inadequate, doubt your sanity, and question your judgment. If you experience any of these feelings, then it means the manipulator has a stronghold over you. Don't ever blame yourself in such situations because it only increases the power the manipulator has. In such instances, remind yourself, you are not the problem, and there is nothing wrong with you. Take a moment to think about the relationship you share with the manipulator and answer the following questions.

- Does this person seem to have unreasonable demands and expectations from me?

- Does he treat me with the respect I deserve?

- Is this relationship well-balanced, or does it only favor him?

- Does this relationship make me feel good about myself?

If your answer is in the affirmative, then there is nothing wrong with the relationship. However, if it isn't, then you are in a relationship with a manipulator. Your answers to these questions will give insight into the kind of person you're dealing with. So, stop blaming yourself, and instead look at the other person.

## Probing Questions

A psychological manipulator will inevitably start making requests. These requests are subtly veiled demands. Often the claims made will be such that you are required to go out of your way to meet his needs. If the claim you're presented with seems to be unreasonable, it's time to shift the attention back onto the manipulator by asking a couple of questions. By doing this, you can judge for yourself whether the person has sufficient self-awareness to realize the unreasonableness of his demands. Here are a couple of probing questions you can ask.

- Is this a request or a demand?

- What will I get if I fulfill this?

- Does this sound fair to you?

- Does this seem reasonable?

- Do you expect me to (restate the demand) do this?

By asking such probing questions, you are placing a mirror in front of the manipulator to check his true nature and intentions. If the manipulator has even a little self-awareness, he will quickly withdraw his demand or even apologize for it. However, it is quite unlikely that an emotional predator will have any awareness about the unreasonableness of his request and might expect you to comply regardless. If the manipulator tries to turn the tables on you and say you are overreacting or are being unreasonable, steer clear of him. Either way, you have your answer.

## Time Is Your Ally

Not only will the manipulator make unreasonable demands but will also expect an immediate answer. By doing this, he is trying to maximize the stress placed on you to exert a higher degree of control over you and on the situation. In such instances, don't play right into the manipulator's trap and buy yourself some time. A suitable response is, "I will get back to you soon," or "I will need to think about it." If you don't respond to this demand immediately, you are preventing him from controlling you. Once you have sufficient time, and can carefully analyze the situation along with its pros and cons. If you feel like it is an unreasonable demand, then you have the right to say "no." This brings us to another point.

## Saying "NO"

A lot of people often struggle with saying "no." You must not only be firm while declining a request but must also do it diplomatically. After all, you do want to prevent the manipulator from creating an unnecessary scene, don't you? You have the right to say "no," and don't let anyone take this away from you. If you allow someone else to control your actions like a puppeteer, you are giving away your power to choose. You can say "no" whenever you want to, and you don't have to feel guilty about it. Don't let the manipulator shame you or make you feel guilty for not complying with his demands.

## Confrontation

An emotional predator, like a manipulator or a narcissist, is essentially a bully. While dealing with a bully, keep in mind that they are often targeting those whom they perceive to be weak or soft targets. As long as you don't take any action, stay compliant, and passive, the bully will always have some control over you. A lot of bullies put up a facade of courage and are often cowardly on the inside. So, once a target starts disobeying them or not complying with their request, bullies tend to back down. This stands right not just for a bully in school, but also in a personal or professional environment. If you ever decide to confront a bully, ensure that you are in a safe and secure environment. Make sure the bully cannot harm you and if required, opt for public confrontations. Having a couple of witnesses around you will be quite helpful. If you need help, ask for it and don't try to do everything by yourself.

## Importance of Consequences

You must not only establish certain boundaries but must also set consequences for the violation of those boundaries. Whenever you feel like someone is violating your limitations, you must deploy a result. This is an important skill, especially while dealing with tricky and unscrupulous individuals.

At times, regardless of all that you do, being around a manipulator can cause irreparable damage to your overall wellbeing. In such instances, you might have to sever all ties and run in the opposite direction. If that's what you need to do for your wellbeing, then don't hesitate. You owe it to yourself, and you deserve better than being manipulated. So, don't sell yourself short and don't subject yourself to manipulative abuse. By following the simple tips given here, you can regain control of your life and prevent anyone from manipulating you.

# CHAPTER 24

# The Role of Defense

ACCEPTANCE INCREASE AWARENESS. The first one is to know what you want and how you feel. When you are connected to yourself, and you really love yourself, you will know if helping somebody or giving something to somebody is going to be good for you. If you are ready to give something to somebody else, you would check if it's coming from inside from you and coming from a genuine loving place and not from a place of guilt, shame, or manipulation. You will know if it is coming from you. And if you genuinely want to do that thing because you don't want to do something. If you feel guilty about it so that you won't have resentment about that person.

So, you should always do something from the kindness of your heart, and if you can't do that, then you should say no. You should try to put yourself first because while you want to do something for somebody else, you should know if that thing is going to be good for you.

# Detach with love Build self-esteem

So, what you should do is to take a scaffold and cut that person out of your life like the way you will cut down a tree. This is what you should do because of the sponge mind effect that your mind has. It tends to soak everything off because of the averaging law. Once negativity steps into your system, it builds up, and it grows like cancer and starts spreading throughout your whole body and through your mind. Moreover, eventually, it will start affecting your habit, affect your way of thinking, and colors your perspective of the world.

So, this can be very dangerous if it is happening over a long time, so you have to build the courage to cut these people out of your life. One thing that you have to acknowledge to yourself is that it doesn't matter who that person is. If somebody is violating your standards and your principles in life, then that person should be cut out of your life. It doesn't matter who it is, whether he's your boss, or your co-workers, or your friends, or your customers. You can cut them out of your life. You could even cut your family out of your life. Most people have problems with their family, and they feel like they can't cut out their family out of their life. Or they feel like they have a very good old friend from Middle School that they have known for decades and they can't cut him. Or they can't cut a client because it's a really important client, and they can't cut their boss off from their work.

So, they give out so many excuses for who they can and cannot cut and why they are certain people in their life that they cannot cut. You have to accept that everybody can be cut out of your life. You need to have boundaries, and you need to have principles as a human being. You hold onto yourself to keep those principles, and you hold onto other people to keep those principles. Now, this doesn't mean that you have to be like a stickler and just cut somebody off for any stupid reason.

It only means that when somebody violates your rules, you can cut them out of your life. Now the closer the person is to you and the more important they are, the more leeway that you can give them. These are people like your mum, your dad, your brother, your sister, or your children. You still need to have boundaries because if you don't set boundaries subconsciously, they will realize that you have no boundaries and people that are close to you will be looking for what they can get away with, and they will keep getting away with more and more things.

So, these toxic people are not really self-developed. They are not operating from a high place of consciousness; they are just running their life like an animal. They have a very animalistic lifestyle, they have low consciousness, and they are just doing the easiest things in life. And those type of people tends to demand more out of life from you. They tend to be a bigger drag. So, for those types of people, you need to set boundaries.

The person that you are going to cut as the Last Resort is your family. As for other people, you should have fewer reservations to cut. Now you should cut somebody out of your life depending on the type of person, their closeness to you, and they're important to you. You should sit down with the person and tell them the problem that you have with them and tell them that it is over don't contact me anymore and I will not contact you again and then just draw a line. You can simply delete the person's number if the person is a casual acquaintance. Don't contact them anymore, block their numbers, block their emails, and block whatever means of communication that they are using for you. Or just stop responding to them. If you are in a relationship like an intimate relationship, then break up with that person.

Breaking up is tough, but sometimes you have to deal with it. If you're in a marriage and the other person is toxic, then consider going for a divorce. Now that may be a nasty process, but it is better than sitting in a toxic marriage for 10 or 20 years. You will not be able to sit that kind of relationship for a long time. So, you should cut the marriage off so that it will not get worse than it is.

If it is in your career, and your business considers quitting your job, or change your job or move to a different department or do a different type of job in the company. If you are the boss or you are self-employed and you have toxic employees, then you can consider firing them. If you have contracts with bad customers, then cut off those contracts and say no to them even though they are going to bring you more clients.

And if the worst comes to the worst and you are in a negative environment, or you are in a really bad part of the city, or you are living in a bad part of the State, or you are in living in a toxic country, then consider relocating. if the worst comes to the worst, you could go to a new city or go to a new country. You need to do that because your environment is very influential on the kind of life that you have and the kind of emotions that you will feel, and the kind of success that you will get. So, take this thing seriously. Now you don't need to cut everybody from your life. Sometimes you might just need to do a reformation.

If somebody is violating your values and you are fed up with all the toxicity, you can sit down that with that person and tell the person what your boundaries are and what your expectations are. Now, this is going to be a difficult task, but you should have that talk and see what happens. Sometimes the talk will change the person, and the person will say, "I don't even realize that I was hurting you so badly, and I don't even realize that I was messing your life up with my toxicity or my negativity. Let me see if I can change something". Sometimes they will do that because they value the relationship, and they know that you will cut them off from your life if they don't.

Sometimes some of the people in a low conscious state that can't help themselves are maybe addicted to drugs or maybe they are depressed, or maybe they have a lot of bad habits, or maybe they don't want to change, and they don't care about changing. This could be the most common cause because these people don't care, they don't want to change and they are not going to accommodate you, so they are going to keep repeating and violating your values, and they won't listen to you, even if you talk to them. They will just continue running on autopilot and be breaking your boundaries.

# CHAPTER 25

# Change Reactions

**B**E PREPARED FOR BACKLASH. This is the part that the person will tell you that you are selfish and he always does things for you, but you never do things back for him and why would he even have someone like you in his life, and all he is asking from you is simple favor, and you turned him down. He may start bullying you or start threatening you, and he will say something like, "I'm never going to do anything for you again." So, he will use a lot of things to throw you off your game, so just expect it to come your way so that you will know how to handle it. You shouldn't get angry or defensive with the person you should see the person as who they are, and just sit back and stay in your truth on what you want and say no to them and only say "I'm sorry you feel that way."

That is one of the best things to say to a manipulated person because after you have seen it, the person won't really have anything again. After all, you are acknowledging that they feel a certain way, and you are sorry that they feel the way they feel. Now you have to remember that all these things are going to take a lot of time. It is going to take a lot of practice on your part, and it will take time for the people around you to get used to it, but the more you continue to love yourself, the more it will become easier for you.

## Be assertive

Then, stand your ground. This is the hardest situation to be in because you are not used to enforcing your boundaries with people. You are not used to standing up for yourself. So, once you know what you want, then telling somebody no might be uncomfortable for you because you have never done it before, but standing your ground is acknowledging that what you are doing is best for you and no one else. It won't make you a bad person, and it won't make you a selfish friend or anything like that, but it only means that you love yourself, and you tend to put yourself first.

You should know that you don't need to explain yourself in a detailed explanation as to why the answer is no. Simply telling somebody, "No, I cannot with a brief explanation is all you need." Anybody that loves you will respect the fact that your answer is no. But somebody that is manipulative or has a fragile ego or does not love you is going to backlash you. So, before the manipulation starts, the guilt may come and then the shame, and then when it doesn't work for them their real abusive behavior comes into play.

## Feed yourself

It is crucial that we all can reach a certain level of emotional intelligence. Your IQ is your ability to think intellectually and logically. Your emotional intelligence (EQ) is based more around your abilities to understand and recognize the feelings and emotions of those around you.

In order to have a high level of emotional intelligence, you need to be aware of what your emotions are and where they started to form. The first way to start to become more emotionally intelligent is to always ask "why." Why is it that you are sad? Angry? Jealous? Scared? When you have these more challenging emotions, always question where they came from and what purpose they are serving.

Ensure that you are separating the emotion from the reaction. If you are angry, you can either react by being quiet or punching a wall. The emotion is the same, but it is the reaction that is positive or negative. Being angry or sad, or any other challenging emotion is not a bad thing. It's when you don't think your reaction through that things can get tricky. Someone with a high EQ knows how to react to their emotions in a healthy way, whereas those with a low EQ often act only on impulses.

Always question your emotions and make sure that you are really looking deep within yourself. Did this emotion develop in the past? Is it a thought process you were taught? Is it something newer that you have developed?

Start to listen better to others as well. Really actively engage in what they are saying and don't just sit there and try to plan out what you are going to say. Listen to their words and the subtext in between.

Voice your opinion and be honest with your feelings. As long as you are not hurting anyone in the process, you should always express how you are feeling. If you bottle up your emotions, then you will only hurt yourself mentally and physically down the line.

Remember to view things objectively. Don't label everything as either "positive" or "negative." There is plenty in between, and you will be able to find both a good and bad side to most things if you look hard enough. Strive for this ambiguity rather than putting everything in one box or the other.

Control your immediate reactions. Let yourself process your feelings for a moment before deciding to react. When you start to improve on this, it becomes that much easier to protect yourself from manipulation.

# Become autonomous and take control

### Establish a clear sense of self

There is a need to know your identity, what your needs and wants are, what your emotions are, and what you are fond of and not fond of. You must learn to accept these and not become apologetic, as these are the things that make you. At times, we dread that in the event of speaking up, we are viewed by others as egotistical and called out for being selfish. Nevertheless, knowing your identity or what you really need in life is not at all an act of selfishness. Self-centeredness is demanding that you always get what you want or that other has always put your needs and wants first. Similarly, when another person calls you out for not following their orders or fulfilling their needs and wants, they are the ones being selfish, not you.

## Say "no" despite the other person's disapproval

The ability to say "no" despite somebody's objection is a solid demonstration. Individuals who can do this are present in reality. Because in reality, there is no way that we can accommodate all of their needs and wants. When this happens, they will become baffled, even disappointed. However, keep in mind that what they are feeling is part of human nature. Most of these individuals would then forgive and forget. Sound individuals realize that getting what you want all the time is not possible, even when the desires are genuine. In any case, when we cannot endure another person's mistake or objection, it really ends up hard stating "no." It winds up more diligently for us to state it or have limits. Manipulators exploit this shortcoming and use dissatisfaction and objection in extraordinary structures to get us to do what they need.

# CHAPTER 26

# Tips for Reading and Analyzing People

THE REAL VAMPIRES; take a moment to imagine a time when the sight of someone sent a chill down your spine. You may not have known why, but you were simply uncomfortable around the person that you were facing. Despite your best attempts to identify the reasoning behind your problem, you found that there was no particular reason that you could discern. The only thing you knew was that you were the only thing afraid of the person in front of you and had no idea how to overcome them.

There was a very good reason for this guttural reaction—your instincts were telling you that something about the other person was not right. You didn't need to know specifics, and all that mattered to you was that your reactions were accurate. This is because all these guttural reactions must do keep you alive. So long as that is managed, your instincts did their job.

When you first look at someone, your unconscious mind goes through all sorts of information to come up with what it assumes is a valid reading of the person. Of course, this all happens beneath your conscious awareness. This means that you are entirely unaware of it as it happens, and yet, you can respond to it without effort. Of course, reacting without second thoughts is a useful trait in a survival setting. You are not trying to rationalize what and why when in a survival setting. You simply react on impulse without wasting valuable time that could be the difference between life and death.

However, if you are not in a life-and-death situation, do you want to be acting on impulse? Will your impulses help you discern whether the person at the interview is lying or simply uncomfortable about something? Or to determine how your partner is feeling during an argument?

There are limitless reasons that being able to rationally understand what is going on in someone else's mind is critical, even if you already have a decent gut reaction. Ultimately, when you can analyze someone calmly and consciously be aware of why you are uncomfortable or what is putting you on-edge, you are better prepared to cope with the problem at hand. This is because you can act rationally. You can strategize on how to better react in the most conducive manner that will allow you to succeed in the situation.

This means that in the modern world, when things are very rarely life or death situations, making an effort to switch to responding rationally and consciously is almost always the best bet. You will be able to tell when someone is setting off your alarm bells because they seem threatening, or because they seem deceptive. You will be able to find out what the problem is to respond appropriately.

# Why Analyze People

Analyzing people is something that is utilized by several people in different capacities. The most basic reason you may decide that you wish to analyze someone is to simply understand them. When you have an in-built technique of understanding others, you will discover that having a cognitive instead of an emotional connection is critical to establishing a true connection with someone else's mind.

Consider for a moment that you are trying to land a deal with a very important client. You know that the deal is critical if you hope to keep your job and possibly even get a promotion, but you also know that it is going to be a difficult task to manage. If you can read someone else, you can effectively allow yourself the ability to truly know what is going on in their mind.

Think about it—you will be able to tell if the client is uncomfortable and respond accordingly. You will be able to tell if the client is being deceptive or withholding something—and respond accordingly. You can tell if the client is uninterested, feeling threatened, or even just annoyed with your attempts to sway him or her, and you can then find out how to reply.

When you can understand the mindset of someone else, you can self-regulate. You can fine-tune your behaviors to guarantee that you will be persuasive. You can make sure that your client feels comfortable by being able to adjust your behavior to find out what was causing the discomfort in the first place.

Beyond just being able to self-regulate, being able to read other people is critical in several other situations as well. If you can read someone else, you can protect yourself from any threats that may arise. If you can read someone else, you can simply understand their position better. You can find out how to persuade or manipulate the other person. You can get people to do things that they would otherwise avoid.

Ultimately, being able to analyze other people has so many critical benefits that it is worthwhile to be able to do so. Developing this skill set means that you will be more in touch with the feelings of those around you, allowing you to assert that you have a higher emotional intelligence simply because you come to understand what emotions look like. You will be able to identify your own emotions through self-reflection and to learn to pay attention to your body movements. The ability to analyze people can be invaluable in almost any setting.

# Early Signs That You Are Dealing with a Predator

### Establish a neutral baseline behavior set

The most important aspect of being able to analyze someone else is through learning how to identify their baseline behavior. If you can do this, you can effectively allow yourself to identify how that person behaves in a neutral setting. Effectively, you will learn what that person's quirks may be.

For example, someone who happens to be reserved or particularly timid is likely to show several common signs of discomfort, even by default. They may cross their arms to shield their body or stand defensively and refuse to make eye contact. As you will learn as you go along through reading, this is a common body language that is regularly exhibited by those who are lying and do not know how to cover their tracks. However, the timid person is probably not lying if their behavior by default involves crossing arms and refusing to make eye contact.

Because people's baseline personality types and quirks vary so drastically from person to person, this becomes a critical first step, and you must make it a point to never skip it. Otherwise, you would assume that any shy person must be trying to deceive you. Getting that picture of baseline personality and nonverbal communication quirks are crucial.

## Identify deviations from neutral behaviors

Once your baseline has been established, you can begin to identify any deviations from it. This means that you can find out which of the behaviors that you are seeing do not match up with what you have come to expect via your initial observations. This stage can occur during all sorts of interactions. You may ask a question and then observe to see what the response will be to determine whether that person is answering truthfully. You can probe and look for signs of discomfort. You can effectively test to see how convincing you are being when you are trying to persuade someone to do something.

## Identify clusters of deviations

Of course, just identifying those individual deviations is not always enough. You must also make it a point to recognize clusters of the deviations to get the true picture. When you master the art of reading body language, you will see that much of human body language can be interpreted in different ways depending on the context. Often, you need to get that context from looking at other behaviors that are occurring in conjunction with the behaviors you are analyzing. For example, there are several behaviors in deception that could have several meanings. Still, as soon as they occur together, you can usually infer that there is some level of deception occurring, which means that you need to proceed with caution.

## Analyze

Finally, as you identify those clusters of deviations from the original, neutral behavioral baseline, you can start to find out what they mean. You can start to trace it back to find out whether or not the person is honest or how they are feeling. When you begin to analyze, that is when you truly get the real snapshot of the thoughts inside the person's mind. You will be able to piece together whether the person has a problem in certain settings based upon seeing general repeated responses. You will be able to tell what is intimidating to them, or what seems to consistently motivate them to keep working toward their goals. In going through this stage, you can start to find out exactly what is needed to influence or manipulate them, if you should choose to do so.

# CHAPTER 27

# The Professional Relationships

**M**ANIPULATION IN THE BUSINESS GLOBAL and paintings cultures often depends upon hidden agendas. It also includes an attempt to coerce or subtly manipulate any other man or woman into giving in or doing what the manipulator desires them to suppose, experience, or do.

- Right here are a few of the most common symptoms of a manipulator at work:

- Superficial appeal and false sympathy

- Negotiations that don't sense truthful, with no win-win solutions

- Verbal intimidation or insincere reward

- Meetings where you unexpectedly leave loaded down with work – with an unfair quantity of monkeys in your lower back

- Passive-competitive behavior

- Human beings kept in the dark about critical selections, with critical information withheld

- The weather of distrust in which there may be a perceived want to tread on eggshells

- Gossiping, putting humans in opposition to one another, spreading rumors

- Less clarity, extra developing confusion

- Bad morale growing at paintings

- Refusal to admit wrongdoing, tries to rationalize, making excuses, and acting surprised whilst confronted

# The Way To Understand A Manipulator

A manipulator might also flatter you because you are the leader and initially appear very supportive of all you do. If they can nurture your acceptance as the ultimate truth, you may properly need you to treat them as a listening ear or a depended on a marketing consultant. If this happens, then you have played right into their fingers. Being on top of things of shaping how you see things might be exceedingly critical to them. Withholding records or spreading snippets of news, primarily based on some 'truths,' however, which create incorrect impressions. In their arms, statistics may be a weapon. Little lies, or 'almost' lies, can be part of their conversations.

Manipulators deliver off mixed messages to the ones around them. They use selective attention, giving it to others whilst it serves their purposes, but regularly absent or giving little attention in different circumstances. For their colleagues, this will be confusing and irritating.

Skilled manipulators don't want to fight their own battles or do their very dirty deeds. They'll search for someone else to do it for them, making sure they're not in the front line. Manipulators will work difficult at positioning themselves advantageously in organizations.

They will rarely take responsibility for their movements or preserve themselves accountable inside the equal manner others do. Additionally, they've 'Teflon' traits. They may be exceptional victims, producing guilt, support, care, and masses of interest. In this way, they make others feel obligated to help them or finish projects that they should be doing themselves. They can evoke the need to be rescued.

Generally, there are adept at sowing the seeds of guilt and confusion, making people feel they're somehow in the wrong or must be doing more. Certainly, they take themselves very seriously and react to the whole thing extremely personal.

## Why Do They Do It?

What do people gain from being manipulators? It's usually right down to getting what they want, something like an object or pay raise, and in the back of that lies a yearning for strength, a need to feel advanced, to constantly be right, to win no matter what it expenses. On the other hand, it isn't about electricity and it's without a doubt all approximately emotional weakness – an excellent issue to recall.

## How Does Manipulation Affect The Place Of Job?

A manipulator can ship a talented workforce to the closest recruitment firm looking for a brand-new task. They pit people against a different situation, set their colleagues up for failure, and force already-strained running relationships over the threshold. Manipulators smash tasks and kill closing dates, alternate the emotional climate profoundly, make their colleagues depressed, and preserve people in a nation of a disappointment for as long as they want. They depend upon secrecy and on different human beings' correct will and reticence.

## Do They Recognize They're Doing It?

Some do, some don't. Whether or not they're self-aware or no longer, a manipulator's behavior is regularly compulsive. They tend to journey themselves up over the years. After they reveal their hand and their behaviors are exposed, they may then determine to move on or need to be moved on. One manner or the alternative matters don't live the identical, it can be a manner of when they have left, there's a few emotional mopping up for all and sundry else to do.

## How To Defuse A Manipulator?

As a leader, how do you address a manipulator? Your first step is to recognize that even as they could look like an effective hazard, most manipulators are very dependent upon others to reinforce their identity. After you and your personnel prevent being fearful, these vulnerable characters can lose the most of their power.

With this attention, you may begin to benefit strength and begin to muster up the courage to act differently.

Your best strategy is to consciously realize what's happening and now not deny it. After you're privy to their approaches, you could push back. Pushing again regularly approach speaking to a person you trust. You will be surprised to discover you're now not the only one who feels that way. If the manipulator is skilled, you've probably been thinking you're going crazy. Identifying and talking to others within the manipulator's field of operation will make it clear, you are sane after all!

It's essential to preserve yourself steady and secure. Don't consider anything that the manipulator says and never supply them any private, work-related, or exclusive situations approximately close to yourself or your role. This can be difficult when you consider that they're notoriously good at producing considerably unique situations that turn into their favor. Just consider any records you deliver them; they may use against you in the near future.

It may be difficult while you're in work, but it enables you to minimize the interactions you've got together with your administrative center manipulator, minimizing the encounters you can't keep away from, quick and expert. If they stop through your desk to the percentage of different people's problems with you, hoping you'll join in, don't get concerned. Gossip is considered one of their biggest weapons, so don't interact with it. If you like, simply say, "I don't do gossip" and shrink back.

## Taking A Robust Stand

As a leader, you might need to take a firm stance on your group's behalf because you're accountable for their nicely-being at work. Be honest with yourself. Let your 'sure' be 'yes,' and your 'no' be 'no.' In the beginning, the manipulator may come off even tougher; however, at heart, those humans are cowards. Don't respond to attempted guilt journeys. As a leader, this is the time while you need to hold your ground and act from your strong integral base.

If you have been studying here and several the situations resonate with you, get in touch to explore how training can help you.

# CHAPTER 28

# Personal Relationships

THE PERFECT PURPOSE OF A MANIPULATOR is to enter into a long-term relationship with their target and to ensure that they have full control over the other individual. This is a very unhealthy relationship because only the manipulator will profit. The equivalent rate of support between the individuals who are in it will be part of a healthy partnership.

But if you're in a marriage that seems like you're always the one that offers, you may be in a relationship with someone dishonest. A manipulative relationship will be hard to identify because the manipulation will be subtler than some other types of relationships toxic.

Psychological manipulation may arise when one tries to create a power imbalance in the hope of taking advantage of another. Manipulation will have several methods that it can manifest, but the one topic that will continue to appear between all is that one individual, the manipulator, will benefit, and the other, the victim, will not and cannot be harmed.

There are occasions when someone ends up in and does not even know a toxic relationship. The partnership may be quite ordinary, without the stress and complications you'll have to encounter in the future while coping with the manipulator. This will form part of the coercion method because it helps the manipulator to reach the target and take control of it without knowing the other individual.

Naturally, the relationship will not begin with the drama or the drain on autonomy or other tactics that the manipulator will then use. When they started, the goal would see them right at the start and go the other way through. A different approach will be taken by the manipulator—one which is slower and slower.

In the beginning, love bombing, and a lot of affection are not going to cause them any problems. When the goal is rooted and often in love, the manipulator begins changing strategies. It is not going to happen overnight and can continue for many weeks so that the objective is not reached before the adjustments are too late. At this stage, the aim has been so spent in and around the marriage that the issues and abuse are overlooked more than in the past.

Apparently, there are some unique indications that indicate a manipulator in your own relationship. It is important to look for these indicators if you are uncertain whether anybody in your marriage is poisonous to you and causing you trouble or if it is a manipulator.

You are urged to leave your comfort zone in many ways. In order to ensure that interests are off track, the manipulator will do this socially, physically, and psychologically. The manipulator can, therefore, be the one with the upper hand and then be the one in charge along the way.

You're going to try to rid your confidence. If we begin having little self-confidence, we will be manipulated more easily, because we are looking for ways to feel better. That's why a manipulator is so quick to ship back our trust to make us feel smaller and never great enough. The operator can take advantage of our weakness.

The secret treatment. That's where you take a small slight from the manipulator to make it a big deal. We will use silent treatment and disregard it to threaten the goal. All e-mails, chances of voice, texts, emails, and more are provided. The manipulator manages to keep everything under control and knows when the silence treatment is over.

The journey with remorse. Neither of us would like to feel guilty of anything, and if we experience that remorse, we'll do all we can to make that shame go away. This is something that the manipulator depends on, and he will accuse and excuse as much as he can for anything they had to do with.

You are denying and glossing about unresolved problems. Unhealthy marriages will flourish with many unresolved disputes as no contact occurs or because the manipulator will not want to settle such conflicts intentionally. That is because it will be easier and better for you if you trick yourself to feel that the conversation has started or finished than first collaborate with you to solve this problem.

We can now understand that this is not so good as to cope with a marriage. None of us would like to be caught up in this sort of relationship in which we feel caught up and like the other individual is always in charge of us. We would like our own lives to be governed. So, without taking full advantage of ourselves, we want to seek one friend who is able to let this happen.

Though, before we go too far, there are some questions we need to ask ourselves in order to help us determine whether we agree that our spouse is a manipulator. When we have been through this here, you will understand quite well whether you have a coercive friendship or not. Some of the measures you can do to defend yourself include recognizing your rights if you are involved in one of these partnerships. It is sometimes difficult to remember how to stand up for yourself when you have had such a friendship for a long time.

Note that irrespective of what you have been instructed by the manipulator, you have fundamental rights to be protect-ed. Such freedoms include the right to respect for others, the right to express some of your opinions, desires, and beliefs, the right to set your own goals without being influenced by someone else and the right to say no to others.

You also have the ability to have a different opinion from another person to help ensure you are psychologically, men-tally, and emotionally secure and can have your own life apart from another person if you choose.

These are the privileges that the manipulator can try in the long run to strip from you. This allows you to maintain the checks you want and ensures that you can do what you say. When you're there in the near future, consider your freedoms, take a deep breath to your friend who's a manipulator, and then try.

You are the only one who controls your life. Stay away. Stay away. Stay away. Then you have to focus on is staying away from the other person. The best thing is always to keep away from a manipulative person.

If this is too late, see if at least you can get a little space from you both. You simply give them another opportunity to learn about you, figure out your vulnerabilities, and find a way to get your future, any time you have to get entangled with someone who is dishonest. Staying away from this person is the first and the only way to protect you from dishonest individuals.

When you begin to feel an incentive to try to improve, go the other direction. Note that the manipulator tries to make you feel bad for you, and they want to help you get back in the marriage and take advantage of you again. Consider your own interest to stay away from the manipulator, and don't drop for the fuck that you want to feel bad and support them.

It's not your fault, mind. Another aspect a manipulator will do is to try to find the right ways to exploit the vulnerabilities. If the manipulator figures out about the vulnerabilities, he will be able to use them to the full and use them against you. It makes it easy to feel inadequate, and often the target ends up constantly punishing yourself for the confusion that the manipulator creates.

This is achieved by the manipulator deliberately. You know you will find ways to avoid culpability. And they know that they can always move the targets so that you can never meet the standards you set, no matter how hard you work and how long you work. It helps them to maintain control of their destination for as much time as possible.

Do not allow this to continue with the manipulator. We want to blame you for shortcomings and to guarantee that you always feel bad, and you stick around and seek validation from them so that you feel better. The implication that none of this, nor anything of which you are accused by the manipulator, is your responsibility. You have just been used to really feel bad, and it is done to make the company and your privileges more likely to be yielded.

The manipulator will lose control over you if you know it is not your responsibility. Know why, yes. Learn how to say no. The partnership manipulator has come to rely on the fact that its goal is always to say yes to everything. They go through lots of information and strategies and make sure they do what they want and say yes.

Knowing how to tell now is one of the fundamental rights we talked about earlier, but it is something we must look into it a little more and widening because it is definitely something that many of us, be it in a manipulative way or not, fail to express on a daily basis.

If we are worried about hurting someone else's feelings, and we think about how someone else's attitude can shift if we refuse to help them, saying yes to someone else can simply make us cry, and often, it takes great bravery. This happens regularly. Imagine, if you deal with a manipulator, how it takes to say no. No strong speech and knowing how to stand for this one will be a valuable skill that will help you to take some power away from and back from the manipulator.

Obviously, they're not going to like that, and you're going

to have to fight to stand up. If you tell 'no' without any remorse, whether or not you work with a manipulator, will be the secret to a freer and healthier life in general.

The target is never better to be in a toxic relationship. It's a whole partnership that will depend on offering what the manipulator needs, and the aim would eventually lose something.

The aim was, however, conditioned to think that this is the appropriate way to do things, so they won't realize they are in a toxic relationship until it's too late. The first step in resolving the problem can be discovering how to recognize when deceit, coercion, and other difficulties arise in your marriage.

It takes time and a great deal of bravery, especially because the aim of that marriage has long been to develop confidence and self-esteem and get them through this difficult time. This takes time and courage. But when it does fall together, and the target actually realizes the connection in which they are and how to strengthen it, they can realize that without a manipulator, everything can really change in their existence.

# CHAPTER 29

# Professional or Personal Relationships

IT IS GOOD TO UNDERSTAND HOW TO INTERACT with different personalities.

Failure to use the communication style that takes care of an individual's emotions, feelings, and behavior can lead to unnecessary disagreements, arguments, and debates.

By knowing to approach each personality in the right way, you can make harmony in your teams at the workplace and improve your interpersonal relationships.

# Interacting with Introverts

- When exchanging greetings put on a smile, but also don't step on their personal space unless you are a close friend, spouse, or close family member.

- Don't stare at them for too long. It will be useful to make intermittent eye contact.

- If you need something from them, it will be useful to make your claim clear other than rambling.

- While trying to get information from them, don't use a lot of small talks or interrupt them while they are talking.

- Be as detailed as possible when explaining something to them and pause to give them time to process and ask a question that they might have.

- Before expecting feedback or an answer from them, give them time to reflect.

- Stick to the topic because they tend to focus on the issue at hand, and any unrelated conversation can make them lose their focus.

- You should understand that they are careful and particular, so don't try to rush them.

- Let them know that everything is under control, especially in the work environment by letting them see the progress you have made before you leave.

- When in a relationship, let them know your specific desires and the goals of the relationship concerning where it is going. Don't just be vague or wishy-washy.

# Interacting with Extroverts

- When exchanging greetings be cordial and brief.

- Maintain direct eye contact when articulating ideas.

- Speak with confidence and be quick.

- Don't beat about the bush. Be straight forward and say directly what you want and why you are there.

- To them, it is a matter of fact and being transparent when getting information.

- Focus on the goal during explanation and do not get into distractions.

- When you propose an idea, support it using reasonable reasons.

- Don't get lost in so many details. Present the main points of your idea.

- When you are working together in a team, stick to the primary purpose, and be efficient.

- In case someone asks you a question, and you do not have the answer ready, let them know that you will get back to them with the solution as soon as possible.

- Avoid being wishy-washy or ague and do not give lame excuses.

- It is good to understand that these types can try to become bossy when under pressure. Assure them that essential steps are being taken to provide a quick solution and try to be humorous to dispel the tension and help lighten the mood.

- In a work-related environment, let them know that things are under control. Appreciate for their time before you leave and do not dilly-dally.

- Don't forget to be warm and friendly in the end as you bid them goodbye.

# Interacting with People with an Agreeable Personality

- Make eye contact when exchanging greetings and don't forget a friendly smile.

- Keep your manner of speaking energetic and friendly and use open gestures.

- With this type, it is good to ask open-ended questions and when they give answers, try to be responsive to them.

- Don't take things too personally, and always try to be prepared for some friendly arguments and friendly debate.

- After presenting the main point and offering some explanation, allow for a session with plenty of questions and engaging conversation.

- In case you are working on a project together, keep the atmosphere conducive and pleasant by coming up with shared interests. This shows that you care.

- Allow them to think aloud, extrapolate, or even digress when giving feedback and answers to a specific issue.

- When explaining things, use personal stories and examples to expound more.

- Don't put pressure on them to make decisions. Always allow for enough time for them to explore options and make up their minds.

- Mention things that can be fun and entertaining when attempting to convince them to adopt a particular idea.

- It is good to keep in mind that these people tend to use humor as a way of breaking tense moments to relax a bit.

- They can become more expressive, more animated and louder, when under pressure. It is also good to know that they can close up completely when under extreme distressing moments.

# Interacting with People with an Open-to-Experience Personality

- Use a friendly tone when exchanging greetings with this type.

- Don't take yourself too seriously. Feel relaxed and get laid-back a bit.

- Don't rush the conversation. Use a cool, calm, and steady tone.

- Avoid being too rush, demanding, and interrupting when soliciting for information from them.

- Make sure to create a conducive environment by taking regular pauses, so that you do not seem to dominate the conversation.

- Show that you are attentive and interested by nodding your head. This also shows that you understand their message.

- Allow for time to reflect and process information after explaining essential ideas and concepts.

- Let them contribute their thoughts on the subject by asking them relevant questions. Actively listen as they make their contribution.

- Understand that they might need more information than you have provided, to understand the idea better, and be of help accordingly.

- While they are talking, try not to finish their sentences even if they get stuck in the middle. Let them turn around their thoughts and continue. They will hate it when you interrupt and finish what they intended to say.

- During conversations, be truthful, open, and honest.

- You need to assure them that it is not a bother when they let you know the help they need and assure them that you will do something about it.

- Always be there to give them support with the issue they have.

- End the discussion in a friendly tone when saying good-bye.

- They can be uncharacteristically critical and angry. This may happen when they are in a situation that has resulted in prolonged stress and pressure. Though it is a rare thing to happen, it is good to understand just in case it happens once in a while.

- Be patient with them. They care less about speed and more about quality. They may reconsider things, revise, and rework to get the results they desire.

- They may get embarrassment from too many compliments and public recognition. It is good to know where to draw the line.

# Interacting with People with Neuroticism

- Their communication style is pretty much similar to that of introverts. It is good to have them here also so that you can grasp them better.

- When exchanging greetings put on a smile, but don't step on their personal space unless you are a close friend, spouse, or close family member.

- Don't stare at them for too long. It will be good to make intermittent eye contact.

- When in a relationship, let them know your specific desires and the goals of the relationship and where it is going. Don't just be vague or wishy-washy.

- If things get stressful, you need to understand that these types can distance themselves from friends. They can get critical and aloof if life feels directionless and

unplanned.
· These types can become stoic and quiet when faced with conflict situations. They may get emotional afterward since they think of the conflict after it has happened.
· It can be frustrating when you interrupt them while they are focusing on an important project or issue. But they will still enjoy humor and friendly banter.
· If you need something from them, it will be good to make your claim clear other than rambling.
· Let them know that everything is under control, especially in the work environment, by letting them see the progress you have made before you leave.

# Conclusion

HEALTHY SOCIAL CONTROL SHOULD BE differentiated from psychological manipulation. Healthy social impact exists among most individuals and is part of positive partnership built on giving and taking. However, dark psychology comes into play when one individual is used in psychological manipulation to the advantage of another. The manipulator intentionally creates a power imbalance and uses the victim to fulfill his agenda.

Given below is a brief overview of some of the important tricks that can be used by covert manipulators to achieve their goals.

It is not necessary that everyone who acts in the following ways can attempt to manipulate you intentionally. Many people have only really bad habits. Regardless, in circumstances where your rights, interests and health are at stake it is important to recognize these behaviors.

Home court advantage a manipulative person can demand that you meet and communicate in a physical space where he or she can exert greater control and dominance. This can be the workplace, house, vehicle, or other spaces of the manipulator in which he feels possession and comfort (and where you neglect them).

Let you talk first to establish your baseline and check for weaknesses as they prospect you, many salespeople do so. They build a baseline on your thinking and behavior by asking you general and inquiring questions, from which they can then determine your strengths and weaknesses. This form of hidden agenda of questioning can also occur on the workplace or in personal relations.

Distortion of facts (deception) excuse me for making it. Met with two. The blame is put on victim for causing their own victimization. Truth-deformation is at its peak. Dissemination or withholding of key information is done to keep you in dark. Overstatement and understatement is rampant.

Overwhelm you with facts and statistics many people enjoy "intellectual bullying" by presuming to be the most experienced and expert in certain fields. They take advantage of you by forcing on you supposed evidence, figures and other details about which you may know nothing. In sales and financial circumstances, in professional meetings and agreements, as well as in social and personal disputes this can happen. The manipulator hopes to drive forward her or his agenda more convincingly, by presuming expert control over you. For no other motive do some people use this strategy than to feel a sense of intellectual superiority.

Overwhelm you with regulations and red tape many people use bureaucracy–paperwork, regulations, rules and by-laws, committees, and other roadblocks to maintain their position and control, while making other lives harder. This method can also be used to postpone the discovery of evidence and the search for truth, mask flaws and shortcomings and avoid scrutiny.

Raising their voice and showing negative emotions many people raise their voices as a means of violent provocation during discussions. The presumption may be that you will succumb to their manipulation and give them what they want if they expressed their voice forcefully enough or show negative emotions. To maximize effect, the aggressive voice is often paired with a strong body language such as standing or excited movements.

Bad surprises some people use bad surprises to obtain a psychological advantage and throw you off balance. In a negotiation environment this can range from low balling to a sudden task that she or he will not be able to come through and deliver in some way. Usually, without warning comes the unwelcome negative information, so you have little time to prepare and combat their advance. The manipulator can request more concessions from you to continue working with you.

Giving you little to no time to decide it is a typical sales and bargaining technique where the manipulator puts pressure on you until you are able to make a decision. By adding stress and pressure on you, you are expected to "crack" and to cede to the demands of the aggressor.

Negative humor It is designed to dig at your vulnerabilities and meant to disempower you. Many manipulators like to make critical comments, often disguised as satire or sarcasm, to make you look inferior and less comfortable. These can include any number of remarks ranging from your appearance, to your older smartphone model, history and qualifications, to the fact that you walked slow and got out of breath in two minutes.

The aggressor aims to exert psychological dominance on you by making you look bad and getting you to feel bad.

Judgmental consistently judge and blame you for making you feel inferior different from the prior conduct in which derogatory humor is used as a cover, here the manipulator chooses you outright. She or he holds you off-balance and preserves her supremacy by continually marginalizing, ridiculing and throwing you off. The aggressor intentionally promotes the illusion that something is always wrong with you, and that no matter how hard you try, you are incompetent and never will be good enough. The manipulator focuses heavily on the negatives without providing concrete and positive ideas or finding practical ways to help.

The silent treatment by purposely failing to respond to your rational calls, text messages, emails, or other questions, the manipulator presumes control by making you wait, and aims to inject doubt and uncertainty into your mind. The silent treatment is a game in which silence is used as leverage.

Pretend ignorance the classic tactic of "playing stupid" is employed by the manipulator. The manipulator / passive-aggressive makes you take on what is her duty by pretending that she or he doesn't understand what you want, or what you want her to do, and gets you to break a sweat.

Some kids use this strategy to delay, stall, and trick adults into doing something they don't want to do for them. This technique is also used by some grown-ups when they have something to conceal or a responsibility they want to escape.

Guilt-Baiting unreasonable blaming is at the heart of this evil technique. Targeting a soft spot of the victim is the key to success for the manipulator.

By exploiting the emotional vulnerabilities and insecurity of the receiver, the manipulator coerces the receiver into ceding to unreasonable demands and requests.

Victimhood social problems are presented in a distorted or imagined manner. The health problems are misunderstood or perceived. Dependencies are ubiquitous.

The objective of manipulative victimhood is often to manipulate the good will of the recipient, the culpable conscience, the sense of duty, or the protective and nurturing instinct to obtain unfair benefits and concessions.

**PLEASE**

*If you liked this book and want more quality books, we will really appreciate your review on Amazon.*
*The number of reviews a book accumulates on a daily basis has a direct impact on how it sells, so leaving a review, no matter how long, helps us keep writing quality books.*

**Thank you so much**

# References Books

Belloc, H. (1967). On. Freeport, N.Y.: Books for Libraries Press.

Bereczkei, T. *Machiavellianism.*

Bladon, R., & Austen, J. *Persuasion.*

Elliott, P. *The sociopath's guide to getting ahead.*

Forsyth, P. *Persuasion.*

Hadnagy, C., Fincher, M., & Dreeke, R. (2015). *Phishing dark waters.* Indianapolis: Wiley.

Heintz, A. (1974). *Persuasion.* Chicago: Loyola University Press.

Joyce, B. (2012). *Persuasion.* Don Mills, Ont.: Harlequin HQN.

Lung, H. (2012). *Mind-sword.* New York: Citadel.

Mills, A., & Raufflet, E. *The dark side.*

Pace, M. *Dark Psychology 101*: Learn The Secrets Of Covert Emotional Manipulation, Dark Persuasion, Undetected Mind Control, Mind Games, Deception, Hypnotism, Brainwashing And Other Tricks Of The Trade.

Simon & Schuster. (1991). Armand Hammer. New York.

Spitzberg, B., & Cupach, W. (2011). *The dark side of inter-personal communication*. New York: Routledge.

Springer Nature. (2020). *Dark Side Of Stand-Up Comedy*. [S.l.].

# Links and Websites

*14 Signs of Psychological and Emotional Manipulation ...* Retrieved 2020, from https://www.psychologytoday.com/us/blog/communication-success/201510/14-signs-psychological-and-emotional-manipulation

*Dark Energy Manipulation* | Superpower Wiki | Fandom. Retrieved 2020, from https://powerlisting.fandom.com/wiki/Dark_Energy_Manipulation

*Dark Light Manipulation* | Superpower Wiki | Fandom. Retrieved 2020, from https://powerlisting.fandom.com/wiki/Dark_Light_Manipulation

*Dark Matter Manipulation* | Superpower Wiki | Fandom. Retrieved 2020, from https://powerlisting.fandom.com/wiki/Dark_Matter_Manipulation

*Dark Psychology 101*: Learn The Secrets Of Covert Emotional ... Retrieved 2020, from https://www.amazon.com/Dark-Psychology-101-Manipulation-Brainwashing-ebook/dp/B013RIQ622

*Dark Psychology & Manipulation: Are You Unknowingly Using* ... Retrieved 2020, from http://drjasonjones.com/dark_psychology/

*Dark Psychology and Manipulation: How to Recognize Mind* ... Retrieved 2020, from https://www.amazon.com/Dark-Psychology-Manipulation-Techniques-Intelligence/dp/Bo84DHWQWD

*Darkness Manipulation* | Superpower Wiki | Fandom. Retrieved 2020, from https://powerlisting.fandom.com/wiki/Darkness_Manipulation

*Light-Darkness Manipulation* | Superpower Wiki | Fandom. Retrieved 2020, from https://powerlisting.fandom.com/wiki/Light-Darkness_Manipulation

*The Dark Psychology of Manipulation: Tactics Used to* ... Retrieved 2020, from https://mindkindmom.com/the-dark-psychology-of-manipulation-tactics-used-to-control-you/

*Minnesota Multiphasic Personality Inventory* (MMPI) https://en.wikipedia.org/wiki/Minnesota_Multiphasic_Personality_